A Woman's Self-Esteem

A Woman's Self-Esteem

STORIES OF STRUGGLE, STORIES OF TRIUMPH

Nathaniel Branden

Jossey-Bass Publishers
San Francisco

Jossey-Bass books and products are available through most book-stores. To contact Jossey-Bass directly, call (888) 378-2537, fax to (800) 605-2665, or visit our website at www.josseybass.com.

Substantial discounts on bulk quantities of Jossey-Bass books are available to corporations, professional associations, and other organizations. For details and discount information, contact the special sales department at Jossey-Bass.

For sales outside the United States, please contact your local Simon & Schuster International Office.

 Manufactured in the United States of America on Lyons Falls Turin Book. This paper is acid-free and 100 percent totally chlorine-free.

Most of the chapters in this book were originally published in slightly different form in *New Woman* magazine; they have been edited and expanded for this volume. The appendix was written for a collection entitled *Feminist Interpretations of Ayn Rand* (edited by M. Gladstein and C. Sciabarra, University Park: The Pennsylvania State University Press, 1999). Copyright © 1999 by The Pennsylvania State University Press. Reproduced by permission of the publisher.

Library of Congress Cataloging-in-Publication Data

Branden, Nathaniel.
    A woman's self-esteem : stories of struggle, stories of triumph / Nathaniel Branden —1st ed.
      p. cm.
    Includes index.
    ISBN 0-7879-4371-1 (cloth : acid-free paper)
    1. Women—Psychology. 2. Self-esteem in women. I. Title.
    HQ1206 .B7   1998
    158.1'082—ddc21   98-9010

FIRST EDITION
HB Printing   10 9 8 7 6 5 4 3 2 1

Contents

Preface   ix

PART ONE: THE BASIC STEPS

1. The Importance of Self-Esteem   3
2. Living Consciously   13
3. Self-Acceptance   19
4. Embracing Our Strengths   25
5. Self-Responsibility   33
6. Self-Assertiveness   39
7. Living Purposefully   45
8. Integrity   53

PART TWO: SPECIAL ISSUES

9. Romantic Love   63
10. Fear of Selfishness   69

11. Jealousy 75

12. Expressing Anger 81

13. Defensiveness 87

14. Success Anxiety 97

PART THREE: EMPOWERING STRATEGIES

15. Trying Something Different 105

16. Knowing Our Boundaries 111

17. Building a Career 117

18. Experimenting in Intimacy 123

19. Choosing Happiness 129

Appendix: Was Ayn Rand a Feminist? 135

References 149

Author's Note 151

About the Author 153

Index 155

To Ashley Victoria Zerah, for the day
when this book may speak to you.

—from Grandpa

Other books by Nathaniel Branden

Who Is Ayn Rand?
The Psychology of Self-Esteem
Breaking Free
The Disowned Self
The Psychology of Romantic Love
The Romantic Love Question and Answer Book
    (with Devers Branden)
If You Could Hear What I Cannot Say
Honoring the Self
To See What I See and Know What I Know
How to Raise Your Self-Esteem
Judgment Day
The Power of Self-Esteem
The Six Pillars of Self-Esteem
Taking Responsibility: Self-Reliance and the Accountable Life
The Art of Living Consciously: The Power of Awareness
    to Transform Everyday Life
Self-Esteem Every Day: Reflections on Self-Esteem
    and Spirituality
Self-Esteem at Work: How Confident People Make Powerful
    Companies (1998, Jossey-Bass)

PART ONE

The Basic Steps

Preface

The book focuses on the basics of self-esteem and the application of self-esteem principles to the everyday lives, conflicts, and strivings of women.

Not in any sense a scholarly work, it is closer to being a primer, with the focus not on humankind in general, as with my previous works, but on women in particular.

The stories that I tell of women's struggles and victories to illustrate my points are taken from my experiences as a psychotherapist. These vignettes are the heart of this book. But in addition, the book contains exercises aimed at facilitating personal development and growth in self-esteem. The emphasis here is on *action*.

Contrary to the claim of some critics, interest in the subject of self-esteem is not "an American fad." It is exploding in one country after another around the globe—from Russia to South Africa to Malaysia. In the fall of 1997,

I was scheduled to do some corporate work in Singapore. In anticipation of my visit, I was invited, in partnership with my wife, Devers, who is also a psychotherapist, to create an evening for the general public on the theme of women and self-esteem. No one knew how many people would come. When the auditorium in which we were to speak was filled—its capacity was six hundred—two hundred additional people were led into an adjoining room where they could witness the event on a television monitor. Another five hundred people were turned away because there was nowhere to seat them. The audience appeared to be about 90 percent women and 10 percent men, and consisted of Singaporeans, Chinese, Japanese, Malaysians, Vietnamese, and a small scattering of Caucasians. The interest in self-esteem was passionate. The most frequently asked question seemed to be some variant of, "How do I find the courage to fight for my own development, against family and cultural pressures?" They did not project that they saw themselves as victims nor did they suggest that man was the enemy. They wanted to know what they could do on their own behalf. What became abundantly clear as the evening progressed was that growth in self-esteem entails a challenge to one's courage. That is one of the themes of this book.

When working on self-esteem, there are two aspects to be considered. One has to do with healing childhood traumas and psychic wounds that have resulted in a damaged sense of self—in other words, the elimination of negatives. The other is the building of positives: learning those practices and ways of operating that result in a strengthened sense of competence and worth. The latter is our focus here.

Whereas the first concern often requires psychotherapy or some other form of professional help, the latter is a domain that a motivated adult can pursue on her own, for example, by studying and experimenting with the ideas and suggestions advanced in this book. Having worked with people for four decades, I am convinced that most of us tend to underestimate what we are capable of accomplishing. We are all more than our problems.

I want to express my appreciation to Alan Rinzler, editor for this project, for seeing the possibilities of this book almost from the first moment of discussion, for his helpful ideas on the book's organization, and for his enthusiasm, which makes working with him such a pleasure.

My second (happy) debt of gratitude is to my wife Devers, passionate supporter and severe critic, who teaches self-responsibility and non-victimhood to her female therapy clients (to her male clients too), and who is my favorite sounding-board for discussions of female psychology.

July 1998 NATHANIEL BRANDEN
Beverly Hills, California

CHAPTER ONE

The Importance of Self-Esteem

Self-esteem is a basic psychological need. And although there is a good deal of talk about it today, there is very little understanding of what the word *self-esteem* actually means.

On a television show, we hear someone say, "When he didn't show up for our date, my self-esteem was *shattered*." In a film about love, seduction, and betrayal among French aristocracy in the eighteenth century, we hear one character say to another, "I wanted you from the first moment I saw you. My self-esteem demanded it." Advertisers tell us that if we use a particular soap, our self-esteem will benefit.

The danger is that a very important idea will become trivialized. And yet, of all the judgments we pass in life, none is more important than the judgment we pass on ourselves.

That judgment has an impact on every moment and every aspect of our existence. Our self-evaluation is the basic context in which we act and react, choose our values, set our goals, and meet the challenges that confront us. Our responses to events are shaped in part by who and what we think we are—in other words, by our self-esteem.

Self-esteem is the disposition to experience ourselves as being competent to cope with the basic challenges of life and as being worthy of happiness. It consists of two components: (1) self-efficacy, that is, confidence in our ability to think, learn, choose, and make appropriate decisions and (2) self-respect, that is, confidence in our right to be happy—confidence that achievement, success, friendship, respect, love, and fulfillment are appropriate for us.

"The basic challenges of life" include such fundamentals as being able to earn a living and take care of oneself in the world; being competent in human relationships, that is, able to sustain relationships that more often than not are satisfying to oneself and to the other party; and having the resilience that allows one to bounce back from adversity and persevere in one's aspirations.

To say that self-esteem is a basic human need is to say that it is essential to normal and healthy development. It has survival value. Without positive self-esteem, psychological growth is stunted. Positive self-esteem operates as, in effect, *the immune system of the spirit,* providing resistance, strength, and a capacity for regeneration. When self-esteem is low, our resilience in the face of life's problems is diminished. We tend to be more influenced by the desire to avoid pain than to experience joy; negatives have more power over us than positives. If we do not believe in ourselves—neither in our efficacy nor in our goodness (and lovability)—the universe is a frightening place.

To women who are throwing off traditional sex roles, fighting for emotional and intellectual autonomy, pouring in escalating numbers into the workplace, starting their own businesses, invading one formerly male bastion after another, challenging millennium-old prejudices—self-esteem is indispensable. To be sure, it is not all that is needed for success, but without it the battle for self-actualization cannot be won.

For women and men alike, if we do have a realistic confidence in our mind and value, if we feel secure within ourselves, we tend to respond appropriately to challenges and opportunities. Self-esteem empowers, energizes, and motivates. It inspires us to achieve and allows us to take pleasure and pride in our achievements.

High self-esteem seeks the challenge and stimulation of worthwhile and demanding goals. Reaching such goals nurtures good self-esteem. Low self-esteem seeks the safety of the familiar and undemanding. Confining oneself to the familiar and undemanding serves to weaken self-esteem.

The more solid our self-esteem, the better equipped we are to cope with troubles that arise in our careers or in our personal life, the quicker we are to pick ourselves up after a fall, the more energy we have to begin anew. Setbacks will not stop the most self-confident of the women who, in the millions, are now starting their own businesses or otherwise struggling to rise in their profession. Nor will a disappointing marriage or love affair so devastate a confident woman's ego that she will arm herself against intimacy to avoid the possibility of future hurt, at the cost of her vitality.

The higher our self-esteem, the more ambitious we tend to be, not necessarily in a career or financial sense but in terms of what we hope to experience in life—emotionally, romantically, intellectually, creatively, and spiritually. The lower our self-esteem, the less we aspire to and the less we are likely to achieve. Either path tends to be self-reinforcing and self-perpetuating.

The higher our self-esteem, the stronger the drive to express ourselves, reflecting the sense of richness within. The lower our self-esteem, the more urgent the need to "prove" ourselves or to forget ourselves by living mechanically and unconsciously.

The higher our self-esteem, the more open, honest, and appropriate our communications are likely to be, because we believe our thoughts have value and therefore we welcome rather than fear clarity. The lower our self-esteem, the more muddy, evasive, and inappropriate our communications are likely to be because of uncertainty about our own thoughts and feelings, as well as anxiety about the listener's response.

The higher our self-esteem, the more disposed we are to form nourishing rather than toxic relationships. This is because like is drawn to like, and health is attracted to health. Vitality and expansiveness in others are naturally more appealing to persons of good self-esteem than are emptiness and dependency. Self-confident women and men are naturally drawn to one another. Alas, insecure women and men are also drawn to one another—and form destructive relationships.

If you hope to achieve a happy relationship with a man, no factor is more important than self-esteem—yours and his. There is no greater barrier to romantic success than the deep-seated feeling that one is unlovable. The first love affair we must consummate successfully in this world is with ourselves. Only then are we ready for a relationship. Only then will we be fully able to love, and only then will we be able fully to let love in—to accept that another person loves us. Without that confidence, another person's love will never be quite real or convincing to us, and in our anxiety we may find ways to undermine it.

When a woman has good self-esteem, she tends to treat others well and to require that they treat her well. She is clear about her boundaries and about what is and is not acceptable behavior in the man of her choice. She does not accept ill treatment merely because she is in love. She identifies love with joy, not suffering. She feels *worthy* of love, just as she feels *worthy* of success in her career.

Women who are struggling to build a more positive self-concept sometimes ask, "Do men *want* self-esteem in a female?" I answer, "Men who have a decent level of self-esteem do value it in a woman; they do not want a frightened child for a partner. And what would a woman of self-esteem want with a man so insecure that her confidence scared him?"

I want to stress that self-esteem is an intimate experience; it resides in the core of one's being. It is what I think and feel about myself, not what someone else thinks or feels about me. I can be loved by my family, my mate, and my friends, and yet not love myself. I can be admired by my associates and yet regard myself as worthless. I can project an image of assurance and poise that fools almost everyone and yet secretly tremble with a sense of my inadequacy. I can fulfill the expectations of others and yet fail to live up to my own. I can win every honor and yet feel I have accomplished nothing. I can be adored by millions and yet wake up each morning with a sickening sense of fraudulence and emptiness. Think of world-acclaimed rock stars who cannot get through a day without drugs. To attain "success" without attaining positive self-esteem is to be condemned to feeling like an impostor anxiously awaiting exposure.

The acclaim of others does not create our self-esteem. Neither does erudition, marriage, or parenthood; nor do material possessions, philanthropic endeavors, sexual conquests, or face-lifts. These things can sometimes make us feel better about ourselves temporarily or more comfortable in particular situations. But comfort is not self-esteem.

Over three decades of study and of working with people as a psychotherapist have persuaded me that the key virtues or practices on which healthy self-esteem depends are living consciously, self-acceptance, self-responsibility, self-assertiveness, purposeful living, and personal integrity. In *The Six Pillars of Self-Esteem*, which I regard as the climax of my work in this field, I examine the meaning of each of these practices in detail. Here I will confine myself to a few broad fundamentals.

To live consciously is to respect the facts of reality without evasion or denial; to be present to what we are doing while we are doing it; to seek to understand whatever bears on our interests, values, and goals; to be aware both of the world external to self and also the world within.

To be self-accepting is to own and experience, without denying or disowning, the reality of our thoughts, emotions, and actions; to be respectful and compassionate toward ourselves, even when we do not admire or enjoy some of our feelings or decisions; to refuse to be in an adversarial or rejecting relationship to ourselves.

To be self-responsible is to recognize that we are the author of our choices and actions, that we must be the ultimate source of our own fulfillment, that no one exists to serve us, that no one is coming to make our life right for us, or make us happy, or to give us self-esteem.

To be self-assertive is to honor our wants and needs and look for their appropriate forms of expression in reality, to treat ourselves with decent respect in our encounters with others, to be willing to be who we are and allow others to see it, to stand up for our convictions, values, and feelings.

To live purposefully is to take responsibility for identifying our goals, to perform the actions that will allow us to achieve them, to keep ourselves on track and moving toward their fulfillment.

To live with integrity is to have principles of behavior to which we remain loyal in action; to have congruence between what we know, what we profess, and what we do; and to keep our promises and honor our commitments—to walk our talk.

In self-esteem groups I have conducted, I saw people transform their lives by learning how to integrate these practices into their daily activities. And, in the process, I often saw "neurotic symptoms" fall of their own weight, as egos grew stronger and healthier.

Throughout history, self-esteem has not been a trait that most cultures have prized in women. (They rarely prized it in men either, but that's another story.) "Femininity" has been identified with passivity, not assertiveness; with compliance, not independence; with dependence, not self-reliance; with self-sacrifice, not self-celebration. To challenge this traditional view of womanhood and to uphold a vision that honors woman's strengths and potentials is itself an act of self-esteem.

If self-esteem is an essential of personal fulfillment, how is it achieved?

In the chapters ahead, I will explore what authentic self-esteem depends on, insofar as it depends on our own actions, and why that is so. I will examine some of the most prevalent misconceptions about self-esteem, such as the notion that it is a gift one can receive from others. I will address the issue of what you yourself—as an adult woman—can do on your own behalf and why primary responsibility for the level of your self-esteem belongs to you and can only belong to you. I will look at some of the beliefs and practices that affect self-esteem either positively or negatively, causing it to rise or fall. I will look at capabilities you may not know you possess. Helping you strengthen your self-esteem—supporting you to fight for the best within you—will be the basic goal here.

CHAPTER TWO

Living Consciously

S ome years ago, Serena, a management consultant, said to me, "I think there are very few major surprises about the man you marry—if you pay attention from the beginning. Through their behavior, most people announce who and what they are pretty clearly. Trouble is, often we don't care to look. Or we're lost in wishful thinking. Possibly we're controlled by our need or our loneliness. We create a fantasy and then get angry with our husband because he's not the fantasy—which he never pretended to be. But if we're willing to look without blinders, if we're willing to see everything that's there to be seen—and if we still love passionately—that's what I call mature romantic love."

I perceived her as a woman of extraordinarily high self-esteem, and one of the reasons was revealed in her statement. She was a person who lived consciously. She exhibited respect for reality. She operated with a high level of awareness. No practice is more self-empowering, and it is not difficult to see why. Living consciously is both a cause of self-esteem and an effect. The more you live consciously, the more you trust your mind and respect your worth. The more you trust your mind and respect your worth, the more natural it feels to live consciously.

If (in effect) we date unconsciously, marry unconsciously, and interact with our partner unconsciously, there will be two predictable casualties: the first will be to our self-esteem, and the second will be to our relationship.

"But what about romance?" a woman in psychotherapy asked me. "Where's the excitement if you're that conscious of everything?" "You mean it's not exciting if you know what you're doing?" I responded, and she smiled sheepishly.

The fact is, many people do act as if consciousness were undesirable. Not only because operating consciously requires an effort they may not care to expend but also because heightened awareness can bring us into contact with facts we prefer not to face. If we prefer to ignore the danger signals Mr. Wrong is emitting, then we can suffer the drama of a new romance, followed by the drama of shock and disillusionment, followed by the drama of bitterness and grief, followed by the heady excitement of playing the story all over again with some new Mr. Wrong. Audiences often laugh—with the shock of recognition—when I point out this pattern. Someone called out once, jokingly, "Who wants to give up the thrills and the heartache?" The answer is: women who know that love and happiness are better served by sight than by blindness.

Sometimes our insecurities make the exercise of consciousness difficult. "If I were willing to admit what I know and not kid myself," a woman in therapy said to me, "I could never remain with Walter. But I'm scared I won't be able to do any better, so I shut my eyes and make myself stupid." Another client, Elsie, who was farther along in her therapy, announced proudly, "I met this terribly attractive guy in the office, and we went out for coffee. The way he talked about women he had been involved with told me this is not a man who likes women. So I had to make a choice: to proceed against that knowledge and set myself up for future pain or drop him right now. I decided I've had enough suffering in my life. I told him very nicely I wasn't interested."

In addition to my psychotherapy practice, I work as a consultant to business organizations. At every level of an organization it is easy to see who is operating at peak awareness and who is mentally coasting. You can note it in the questions people ask (or don't ask) and in their hunger to expand the range of their competence (or their avoidance of any nonobligatory effort).

When Marvel, age thirty-four, was hired for a new job in an insurance firm she did everything she could to master what was required of her and kept looking for ways to perform her tasks more efficiently. Beyond that, she sought to understand the wider context in which her work took place so that she would be qualified to move up and not be stuck indefinitely on the level at which she had started. Her basic desire was to *learn*—and thereby to keep growing in confidence, productiveness, and competence.

When Angie was hired by the same firm, she imagined that if she memorized the routine of the tasks assigned to her and didn't attract negative attention, she might hope for security. *Challenges* had no appeal for her. All her thoughts centered on her desire for a hassle-free life. She operated at the minimal level of awareness necessary to carry out her basic duties, contributing nothing of her own. Her interests, she thought, lay not in what she did at work but in what she did *after* work—socializing with her friends. Her gaze rarely strayed from her workstation. She felt no curiosity about how her job fitted into the overall context of the company. She kept a small clock in front of her so that she would know precisely when it was five o'clock and time to go home. When she was confronted by her supervisor with mistakes she had made, she typically alibied and inwardly seethed. But when Marvel was promoted and she was not, Angie felt bewildered and resentful.

Apart from the practical consequences for their careers, Marvel's and Angie's policies necessarily have consequences for the women's self-esteem, in the first instance strengthening it and in the second eroding it.

Angie, of course, represents an extreme, but her basic pattern is one that can be found in varying degrees. We can be significantly more conscious in the workplace than Angie, yet nowhere near our potential. If 10 is optimal consciousness and Angie is, say, a 2, where would you place yourself?

A powerful technique for stimulating self-awareness, self-development, and self-healing is sentence-completion work. In my therapy practice I typically give homework assignments in which—if the project is to learn to operate at a high level of awareness—I ask people to write six to ten endings, each morning for a week or two, for the following stems:

> If I were to bring 5 percent more consciousness to my daily activities—
>
> If I were to bring 5 percent more consciousness to my choices and actions—
>
> If I were to bring 5 percent more consciousness to my important relationships—
>
> The hard thing about operating consciously is—
>
> The rewards for operating consciously might be—
>
> I am becoming aware—

When doing this exercise one does not stop to think (rehearse, censor); one writes as rapidly as possible—the only assignment being to write a grammatical completion of the sentence stem. If you get stuck, *invent*. Write *anything* but write *something*.

If you choose to do this exercise daily for the next two weeks, you may be astonished at how much you learn—and what possibilities open for you.

CHAPTER THREE

Self-Acceptance

Without self-acceptance, self-esteem is impossible. If I am locked in a pattern of self-rejection, my personal growth is stifled—and I am not going to be happy.

But what self-acceptance means is far from self-evident. Some years ago, when I was writing *How to Raise Your Self-Esteem*, I found that this subject required the longest chapter. Here is the essence of the issue.

"To accept" *is to experience reality fully, without denial or avoidance.* This is different from merely "acknowledging" or "admitting" in the abstract. It is also different from liking, admiring, or condoning. I can accept the reality of things about myself that I do not like, admire, or condone at all. Here is a simple example.

Suppose I am feeling envious of my friend, who has a better job and a more satisfying love life. To practice

self-acceptance does not mean to like or enjoy my feeling of envy. It means to own and experience the feeling as mine, not to deny or disown it. It also means to retain a sense of my value, even though I do not like what I am feeling right now. I respect facts, in this case the fact that I am feeling envy. I allow myself to experience the feeling, and I examine it. My concern is not with "judging" myself but with being aware. Perhaps among other things, I will learn that I have wanted something more than I knew, and I will need to think about that.

Not uncommonly, when I bring this kind of consciousness to unwanted feelings—envy, or rage, or fear, or sadness, or some other discomfiting emotion—such feelings often melt and give way. But even if they don't without more self-work, this is where I begin; I cannot evolve out of my unwanted feelings if I cannot accept having them. I cannot leave a place I have never been.

So, focus on the unwanted feeling, breathe gently and deeply, as if opening to allow it in—don't fight or resist it—be aware that you are more and bigger than any feeling of yours—and thereby create a context in which change and growth can happen.

Or take the case of Paula, a mother of four children. Her husband had taken the children for an outing, giving her a few hours of delicious freedom. For a few hours no one wanted anything from her; she did not experience

her normal feeling of being pulled in different directions; she wondered if she should feel guilty for enjoying herself so much. The thought occurred to Paula in a flash that if her husband and children were somehow to "disappear," she would be free to belong to herself again. Then she was aghast. How could she have such a terrible thought? She slammed her consciousness shut tight against it. She did not know that everyone has thoughts of this kind. So she told herself, "What kind of woman must I be? I am a bad person; I am a bad mother." She plunged into self-rejection.

What would it mean to be self-accepting instead? She would allow herself to experience the thought while knowing it was only temporary and not her real conviction. Still, in the moment it expressed an aspect of herself—and she would own that. She would examine whether it pointed to a genuine frustration that needed to be examined and dealt with. Her concern would be not with evaluating but with understanding. She would be a friend to herself. She would not permit an involuntary thought to be a reflection on her self-esteem.

Apply this policy to yourself the next time you have a thought for which you start to feel guilty.

The same principle applies to actions. I am thinking of a client, Alice, age thirty-eight, who said she hated to think of the person she had been in her twenties because that person did drugs, slept with men whose names she could not remember, and generally abused herself. I asked her if she had ever tried to enter into the consciousness of that younger self, tried to understand where she was coming from, what needs she was struggling to satisfy, what her context was that made her behavior seem desirable. "Do you mean condone all that?" she demanded indignantly. "No," I answered. "I mean understand it. Accept that at the time those behaviors were an expression of you. The behaviors were self-destructive; they hurt your self-esteem; no argument. Does that mean that the way to protect your self-esteem now is to disown the girl who committed them—like a disapproving parent? To refuse to look at the period of your life or to accept that that girl was *you* or to offer her any compassion? As long as you hate and reject a part of who you are—or were— you remain in an internal war, and there is no way your self-esteem will not suffer."

Late in therapy, when Alice had looked beyond this problem, she said, "When I look back and accept that this was me, it's funny, I feel stronger and cleaner because I'm not fighting facts."

What would it mean to apply this practice to your own experience? Think about that.

When we accept our experience, without necessarily liking it, we ally ourselves with reality and thereby empower ourselves. When we don't, we set ourselves against reality and become weaker.

Unfortunately, when we were children many of us were subtly or not so subtly encouraged to pretend that we didn't think what we thought or didn't feel what we felt, when what we thought or felt was disturbing to grown-ups. We were rewarded with "love" and approval for slashing away pieces of ourselves. We denied fears, suppressed judgments, buried our anger, disowned our sexuality, and relinquished our aspirations—in order to "belong." Having learned this pattern of self-rejection, we go on doing it throughout life to *win favor in our own eyes.* Our aim is self-protection, but the result is self-alienation.

This is the pattern we must learn to reverse. We must give up the notion that there is a virtue in self-repudiation. Self-esteem is intimately tied to a relentless respect for facts, *including facts about our own person.* This is why self-acceptance is so important.

I have seen many women (and men) struggle with personal problems and progress agonizingly slowly, if at all, because at the deepest level of the psyche they are profoundly self-disowning and self-rejecting. And without that policy being challenged, self-healing is close to impossible. These are people for whom new learnings never seem to stick, and apparent advances end up being transitory and impermanent.

Self-acceptance is my refusal to be in an adversarial relationship to myself. It is one of the indispensable building blocks of healthy self-esteem.

Here is a basic sentence-completion exercise to facilitate self-acceptance. Every day for a week or two, write six to ten endings for each of these stems:

If I were 5 percent more self-accepting—

If I were 5 percent more accepting of my thoughts—

If I were 5 percent more accepting of my feelings and emotions—

If I were 5 percent more accepting of my past mistakes—

If I dealt with myself more compassionately—

When I treat myself with rejection—

I am becoming aware—

CHAPTER FOUR

Embracing Our Strengths

"If I were to own my intelligence fully," a woman said in one of my therapy groups, "my family would repudiate me." We were exploring some of the difficulties in practicing self-acceptance in spite of its importance to self-esteem.

Another woman said, "If I were fully to experience and admit my excitement, I would have to face the loneliness of seeing that no one shares my feelings."

"If I were fully to admit my capabilities," said another, "I'd end up taking on even more responsibilities than I do now."

"If I were to fully own my passion," said another, "I'd have to admit the boredom of my marriage—and then what would I do?"

"If I were to own my sexuality," said another, "my husband would be frightened."

25

"If I were to own my spirituality," said another, "I don't know where that would lead me; it's unfamiliar territory; I'd feel completely isolated."

"If I were to admit how much I secretly like myself," said another, "I'd become an instant orphan—because Mother couldn't handle it."

Self-acceptance is essential to self-esteem. To "accept" is to experience the reality fully rather than denying and disowning it. It's easy to understand why many people have difficulty accepting their own *negative* thoughts, feelings, and action. But, as we see in the statements quoted, the challenge of self-acceptance applies equally to *positives*—to strengths and assets that we may be tempted to deny and evade because they provoke anxiety and disquietude. For some of us, accepting the best within us may be a more difficult challenge than accepting our "dark side."

As a general rule, any expression of the self that we have the ability to experience, we also have the ability to disown. For example, just as a woman can refuse to accept her dark thoughts, she can refuse to accept her flashes of deep wisdom. Just as she can refuse to accept her excessive materialism, she can refuse to accept her spirituality. Just as she can disown her sorrow, she can disown her joy. Just as she can repress the memory of actions she is ashamed of, she can repress the memory of actions she is proud of. Just as she can deny her ignorance, she can deny her knowledge. Just as she can refuse to accept her limitations, she can refuse to accept her potential. Just as she can conceal her weaknesses, she can conceal her strengths. Just as she can deny her feelings of self-hatred, she can deny her feelings of self-love. Just as she can disown her body, she can disown her mind.

As I wrote in *How to Raise Your Self-Esteem*, "Our strengths or virtues can make us feel alone, alienated, cut off from the common herd, a target for envy and hostility, and our desire to *belong* can overcome any desire to actualize our highest potential" (p. 62).

If a woman can pretend to be *more* than she is, denying her shortcomings, she can also pretend to be *less* than she is, denying her capabilities. She may disown her intelligence, perceptiveness, certainty, strength, vitality, or passion. She may reject the very traits most worthy of being prized.

She may do so in the name of protecting other values of hers, such as her marriage (to a husband who might feel threatened by her strength) or her relationship with family or friends (who might feel intimidated by her or envious). She may do so because fully owning her capabilities may entail responsibilities of which she is frightened. She may do so because her limited self-concept may not be able to accommodate some of her best traits—so, to protect her equilibrium, she exiles them from awareness.

One can have understanding and compassion for such acts of disowning. One can acknowledge that a woman's socialization often encourages the disowning of her power. And yet, self-rejection is self-rejection—and the consequences for self-esteem are severe. When we deny and slash away pieces of who we are, whatever the reasons, the result is a wounded and impoverished sense of self.

"What I'm beginning to see," said Claire, a psychotherapist married to Tim, also a psychotherapist, "is that this whole issue comes down to telling the truth. At meetings with colleagues I present myself as less knowledgeable than I am in order to make Tim look good. I don't do what I could do to build a great office practice. I grew up believing too much brains or energy in a woman is undesirable. Tim isn't demanding this act of me; I'm demanding it of myself because I'm frightened to find out what would happen and whether he would still love me if I fully expressed who I am. Meanwhile, I'm living a lie. And it's eroding my self-respect."

"Really to admit your intelligence—I mean, all the way," said Shirley, an assistant to a film producer, "is a responsibility. It's not so much that others expect more of you; you expect more of yourself. But the truth is, I like feeling a little bit helpless. It's how my family has always seen me. My boss says I haven't touched my potential and that I could have a fabulous career. That idea makes me anxious. It's not how I think of myself. And yet the truth is, I know she's right. And that means my family is wrong. Do I have the strength to handle that? And if I don't find the strength, now that I've admitted what I've admitted, how do I face myself?"

It takes courage to know and fully to be who we are. It takes honesty to admit, even in the privacy of our own minds, "I can do things others don't seem able to do," or "I have a better mind than anyone else in my family," or "I want more out of life than the people around me do."

When a person in a relationship begins to change, the partner is obliged to change also. The reason is that a relationship is a system whose parts are interconnected. If one part changes and another part doesn't, the system goes into disequilibrium. Frictions and tensions develop.

After several months of therapy, Claire remarked, "As I'm learning to 'come out' more, there's a period of adjustment for Tim fully as much as for me. For one thing, he has to learn not to interrupt. More important, he's learning to handle the fact that I'm making as much money as he is, and might end up making more. He's happy—perhaps because he sees that I am, and also, perhaps, because he sees that I don't hold him responsible for my past reticence. I take responsibility for what I've done to myself and for the changes I need to make."

Reporting on her progress, Shirley said, "Except for one sister who has become my enthusiastic supporter, my family isn't too happy with the new me. They make a lot of jibes and petty sarcastic remarks about 'getting too big for my britches.' I don't see them as often as I used to. I still miss them sometimes, but I would miss myself more if I hadn't decided it was time to own who I am. Maybe they'll adjust; maybe they won't. I can't let that stop me."

It takes integrity to place relationships in jeopardy by being true to the best within ourselves. It takes wisdom to know that the relationships that are right for us will grow stronger if we own our power, and relationships that are toxic are better ended sooner than later.

But let us not be self-deceiving. Growth often entails risk and pain. The reward is pride in what we have chosen to become. I have never known a woman who, having embraced the best within herself, later expressed regret at having done so. But I have known many women who, having avoided this choice, sentenced themselves to a lifetime of regret.

Here is a sentence-completion exercise to carry this work further:

If I were 5 percent more accepting of my intelligence—

If I were 5 percent more accepting of my sexuality—

If I were 5 percent more accepting of my spirituality—

If I were 5 percent more accepting of my excitement—

If I were willing to breathe deeply and feel my own power—

I am becoming aware—

CHAPTER FIVE

Self-Responsibility

Obedience. Conformity. Good manners. Church attendance. Early in this century these were the values that most parents were most eager to instill in their children, according to a study done then. But our priorities have changed. When the study was repeated during the 1980s, none of these items figured prominently. Instead, one of the top values parents said they wanted to teach was self-reliance. What this reflects is a new awareness of the qualities needed for successful adaptation to an increasingly complex and unpredictable world. This shift of consciousness is important to all of us, but it is especially important to women. Women are realizing that self-reliance is not a male prerogative.

Unfortunately, many women still feel that there is more "power" in passivity and helplessness than in taking active charge of their own destiny. Often their socialization encourages this belief. They may dream of a "rescuer" who will make the world right for them, who will "give" them happiness, fulfillment, and self-esteem. As one of my clients remarked wryly, "That's what, in effect, my mother promised me."

Yet neither self-esteem nor personal efficacy can be received as a gift from others. It is generated from within or not at all. And among the ways it is generated, none is more important than learning and practicing self-responsibility. In my psychotherapy practice I see over and over again the tremendous power that flows from an individual's willingness to accept rather than evade responsibility for her existence. Self-responsibility entails

Taking responsibility for our actions

Taking responsibility for our decisions

Taking responsibility for the fulfillment of our desires

Taking responsibility for our choice of companions

Taking responsibility for how we deal with people—at work and in our personal life

Taking responsibility for how we treat our body

Taking responsibility for our happiness

The practice of self-responsibility entails taking appropriate care of oneself, in all those matters open to one's choice. It does not mean accepting responsibility for that which is outside our control. We are not responsible for the actions of others, but we are responsible for our own actions.

Veronica was a dental hygienist whose lover of seven years was repeatedly and almost compulsively unfaithful. "If only Stan would come to therapy," she complained, "but he won't. What's the matter with men anyway?" I asked when he first gave evidence of infidelity, and she said that almost from the beginning she caught him in flagrant lies about his relationships with other women. She wept and suffered but never seriously challenged his behavior. Her constant refrain was, "Everything would be so wonderful if only he would change." It took several difficult months of therapy before she was willing to take responsibility for *choosing* Stan for a mate and for *choosing* to remain with him and to sanction his behavior. As the next step in her progress she gave him an ultimatum: stop his flings and seek professional help or the relationship would end. When she saw that he refused to take her ultimatum seriously, she left him. "It's agony," she admitted to me. "I still miss him. But recovering heroin addicts miss heroin for a while, don't they? The good thing is, I don't feel like a victim. I feel like a grown-up in charge of my own life." The refusal to be a victim in situations where real choices do exist is one of the meanings of self-responsibility.

Henrietta was a graphic designer who helped support several able-bodied members of her family. She was constantly on call for their many crises, and she consulted me because of depression, complaining that she had no life of her own. "How can I take care of myself," she asked bitterly, "when everyone is always needing me?"

I suggested we do some sentence-completion work and gave her the stem, "The good thing about being everyone's caretaker is—" and asked her to keep repeating that stem, ending the sentence a different way each time.

Her endings included, "I feel important; I don't have to think about myself; I don't have to deal with my pain; I don't have to face my fears; I get to feel noble; I get to be a martyr; I don't have to solve any of my problems; I get to suffer and complain a lot."

Then I gave her the stem, "If I took more responsibility for my own life—."

Her endings included, "I'd need courage; I'd say no when I wanted to say no; I'd belong to myself; my family would be shocked; I'd have to look within; I wouldn't try to lose myself in other people's problems; I would tell you about my fears; I would tell you about my frustrations; I would tell you what I want for myself but have been frightened to go after."

One of the ways we can avoid self-responsibility is by taking on responsibilities that are not properly ours, thus concealing self-avoidance under the mantle of "virtue." "It's so much easier," observed Henrietta in astonishment, "to live for others rather than for oneself. Now, every time I treat my needs with respect, I feel pride."

Most of us will recognize that we are more self-responsible in some areas and less so in others; sometimes we operate more as an adult, sometimes more as a child. Looking at an area where we know we are not as self-responsible as we need to be, it is useful to ask ourselves, What would our behavior look like if we chose to be more responsible here? In practicing that behavior, we empower ourselves. In expanding the range of our self-responsibility, we build self-esteem.

By way of getting started, here is a two-week program you may find useful. For the next fourteen days, in the morning, write six to ten endings, as rapidly as you can, for these stems:

> If I operate 5 percent more self-responsibly today—
>
> If I operate 5 percent more self-responsibly at work—
>
> If I operate 5 percent more self-responsibly in my relationships—
>
> I avoid self-responsibility when I—

Sometimes I make myself helpless when I—

If I accept full responsibility for my own happiness—

I am becoming aware—

Don't worry about repetitions among your endings from day to day. If you do the exercise, new possibilities of personal power will present themselves to you.

CHAPTER SIX

Self-Assertiveness

When we have good self-esteem, self-assertiveness tends to follow as a natural consequence. And when we are appropriately self-assertive, we strengthen our self-esteem. The relationship is reciprocal. One of the ways we can build self-esteem, then, is by learning to honor our wants, needs, values, and thoughts—and by seeking appropriate ways to express them in the world.

Self-assertiveness means my willingness to stand up for myself, to be who I am openly, to treat myself with decent respect in my encounters with others. It means I don't fake who I am—misrepresent my values or belief or perceptions—to win your approval.

This self-assertiveness has nothing to do with pushing to the front of the line, or demanding to always be the center of attention, or recognizing no one else's rights, or being indifferent to the interests of others, or babbling about one's feelings indiscriminately, regardless of the situation.

One of the most self-assertive women I have ever known is also one of the kindest and most generous. But she is unwilling to live underground—unwilling to hide her intelligence or her convictions or her passions. She treats her needs and goals as important—not necessarily important to others but important to herself.

Women often disown their strengths because they are afraid that to express them will lead to loss of love. Janine adored her father and felt adored by him until she reached age twelve. Up to that time, she had responded to all his pronouncements as wisdom incarnate, and he basked in her vision of him. Then, as her ability to think developed, Janine began to ask challenging questions. She became more self-assertive, and in disorientation and fear, he retreated from their relationship, silently detaching from her and over time becoming critical and scornful. She was left to feel abandoned and discarded, and as a young woman to struggle with the questions, *To keep love, do I have to deny what I see and know? Is too much consciousness the enemy of relationships?*

Many women wrestle with these questions, and some choose to relinquish their intelligence, unaware that they are also relinquishing self-esteem. Self-assertion begins with the act of exercising consciousness—of seeing and thinking. If we retreat from this challenge, inevitably we wound our self-esteem.

Never get involved with a man who is not a friend to your intelligence. If you do, the price you may pay for his "love" is loss of love of yourself.

Self-assertiveness takes many forms: asking for a raise and offering good reasons why you deserve it; expressing a moral, political, or aesthetic conviction that may not be shared by your listeners; paying an enthusiastic compliment that genuinely reflects your values; informing a friend that her exploitative behavior is unacceptable and declining to cooperate with it; recommending a book or movie you love; comfortably acknowledging your needs and vulnerability; being honest about your anger; asking questions straightforwardly without the need to pretend you already "know"; treating your ideas with respect and fighting in appropriate ways for their acceptance; refusing to laugh at someone's tasteless joke; naturally and nonbelligerently expressing your loves and enthusiasms; sharing your excitement; letting others hear the music inside you.

Healthy self-assertiveness is not hostile, abusive, or sarcastic. The latter are typically low-self-esteem behaviors and should not be confused with what I am recommending. We need judgment about what feelings we will express under what circumstances; to exercise such judgment is not to sacrifice self-assertiveness but to be intelligent about its exercise.

I recall working in therapy with a woman whose notion of self-assertiveness was tied exclusively to defiance and rebelliousness. As a teenager Carla had felt her survival depended on saying no to the values of her parents, and she had been locked in a posture of No! as her basic response to the world ever since. Now in her mid–thirties she was confronted with the awareness that blue jeans, combat boots, and a succession of dead-end jobs and dead-end lovers could not conceal the impoverishment of her inner life.

"The ability to say no is important," I remarked to her, "but self-assertiveness is tested not by what we are against but what we are for." "I've never been *for* anything," Carla answered sadly.

I decided we would do sentence-completion work. I would give her an incomplete sentence, or a series of incomplete sentences, and ask her to keep repeating it aloud, each time with a different ending, without thinking, planning, or rehearsing.

I gave Carla the sentence stem, "If I said yes when I want to say yes—."

She responded, "If I said yes when I want to say yes, I would see how many opportunities I've been blind to; I would admit all the things I've denied wanting; I would accept friendship when it's offered; I would accept my hunger for contact; I would reach out to life; I would go back to school; I would know how much I want to learn; I would let love out; I would be scared; I might come alive." She looked dazed and astonished at what she heard herself saying.

I gave her another sentence stem. "If I brought more self-assertiveness to my daily activities—."

Her responses included, "I wouldn't hide so much; I wouldn't see myself as a victim; I wouldn't always be angry; I'd find out who I am; I'd be more honest about my feelings; I'd admit when I'm hurt; I'd admit when I'm lonely; I'd think about making something of myself; I wouldn't stay in a stupid job and blame 'the system,' I'd look for something better; I'd admit I have dreams and ambitions." Carla looked at me, laughed, and added, "I can't believe I said all that." This was the beginning of her breakthrough.

To face our own wants and honor our own values takes courage. We need to come out of our hiding places. We need to participate in life. At first, it may be difficult. But the world belongs to those who persevere.

Here is an exercise to help you work on cultivating self-assertiveness. First thing in the morning, before the business of the day, write six to ten endings, as rapidly as possible, for each of the following sentence stems:

If I bring a higher level of self-assertiveness to my activities today—

If I treat my thoughts and feelings as important—

If I say yes when I want to say yes and no when I want to say no—

If I ask for what I want openly and with dignity—

I am becoming aware—

Do this exercise, Monday through Friday, for two weeks. Naturally, there will be lots of repetitions among your endings. Don't worry about it. New endings will also emerge. At the end of the first and second weeks, on the weekends, read over what you have written and do six to ten endings for this stem:

If any of what I've written is true, it might be helpful if I—

This exercise should begin to open doors for you—help you to see new possibilities for self-expression. Nothing is won without risk. The choice is yours to gather the courage to walk through these doors.

CHAPTER SEVEN

Living Purposefully

Self-esteem entails an experience of control over our own existence. We have an inner compass that guides us and sets our direction so that the locus of control is felt to be within, rather than somewhere out in the world. In contrast, a person with low self-esteem feels herself primarily under the control of external events, which means the choices and actions of others. She responds to life passively rather than proactively. This difference in life-pattern is a reflection of the degree to which a woman operates *by conscious purpose*.

Our *purposes* organize and focus our energies, and give meaning and structure to our existence. In order to finance my education, I may take a job I do not enjoy; yet I am able to feel in control of my life, even when performing uninspiring tasks, if I hold in mind the wider context and the goal toward which I am moving. In the absence of goals and purposes, I experience myself as essentially at the mercy of chance—my own random impulses or the uncontrollable actions of others. This passivity is incompatible with the experience of self-esteem.

To live my life at the level of conscious purpose, I need to take responsibility for formulating my goals. What do I want to achieve in terms of personal development? What do I want to achieve professionally? What do I want out of my relationships? I need to think about how to get there from here, meaning I need to answer the question, What actions will I need to take to get what I want? In other words, I will need an action plan. Also, I need to monitor my behavior over time to assure myself that I am on track, that my actions remain consistent with my goals and action plans. Finally, I need to pay attention to the outcomes of my actions, to determine whether they are in fact producing the results I intended and envisioned. These policies are enormously self-esteem building, because they generate a sense of competence in the face of life's challenges.

Here are three examples of what the idea of operating purposefully means in action.

In therapy Mary said to me, "I want to be a writer. I've wanted that since I was twelve."

I asked, "Have you ever written anything?"

"No," she replied. "Not since college."

"Have you taken any courses on writing or read any books on the subject?"

"No, not really."

"Do you read much? Try to learn what is good writing?"

"No."

"Do you have any plans for a specific writing project?"

"No."

Mary merely *fantasized* about being a writer. This is not living purposefully and it leads nowhere, except to frustration. I gave her a homework assignment. "I want you to write a several-page answer to this question: If I were to convert my desire to be a writer into a conscious purpose, *what would I need to do?*" A consequence of this assignment was that Mary enrolled in a writing course at UCLA.

Jean was a manager in a small computer firm. She had many ideas on how to make the business grow and how to advance her own career in the process. She also had the enthusiastic support of her bosses. But she was always being sidetracked by the problems brought to her by the people she supervised. "I know it's not really my job to solve their problems; it's their responsibility. But I was raised to think of myself as a caretaker, and it's really hard for me to say no to people. Everyone wants me for something. Often I have to work late, after everyone has gone, to get my own work done."

"If you were to place your own projects and goals first," I asked, "which is what your company wants you to do, in what ways would you need to behave differently with your staff?"

"I would have to hand back to them problems that are theirs to solve. I'd require a higher level of responsibility from them."

"And what might be the obstacle to doing that?"

"Well . . . maybe if I stood up for myself . . . they wouldn't like me?"

"So if you were to require that they be more self-responsible, which is a way of empowering them, they might resent you?"

"Actually, I don't think they would, but that's not the point, is it?"

"Exactly right. The point is, living purposefully can require not only discipline but courage—the courage to honor one's own values and goals, with or without the enthusiastic support of others."

As Jean learned to overcome her fears and bring more purpose and focus to her work, the inevitable occurred: the performance of her department rose—and so did her self-esteem and enjoyment of life.

If people understand the idea of operating purposefully at all, they are most likely to understand it in the workplace. They are least likely to understand its application in the intimately personal arena. The examples given so far involve work; here is an example involving love.

"I would like to be a better partner to Max," said Caroline, who felt herself torn between her love life, her many women friends, and her career as owner of a highly successful flower business. "I really care for him. He complains I don't give us enough time. I'm always in a rush. Or on the telephone."

"What would you like to do differently?," I inquired.

She seemed puzzled by the question. "I'd like both of us to be happier romantically."

"What do you see yourself doing that would make both of you happier?"

"I'd help create a better relationship," she said, a little tentatively.

"Good. If that's your purpose, what actions would you need to take to create a better relationship?"

Clearly this line of questioning had not occurred to her. "I'm embarrassed to admit that I don't know. I know that my purpose at work is to increase sales 20 percent this year, for which you'd better believe I've got an action plan! But I guess I don't really have a purpose for this relationship, just a wish."

Caroline embarked on what she called "an interesting experiment"—to learn what would happen if she brought as much focus and purpose to improving her relationship with Max as she brought to her business activities. This meant, among other things, taking better charge of her time, so that her relationship with Max did not suffer from malnutrition. Today she is successful in *both* areas of her life.

One of the most potent ways of raising self-esteem and thereby gaining more satisfaction is *by converting desires into purposes*. Again, here's how:

Ask yourself what actions you would need to take if your purpose were to achieve your goals in reality (rather than just dream about them).

Design an action plan and begin to implement it.

Monitor your progress and pay attention to the outcomes of your actions. Adjust your plans and behavior when necessary.

Keep yourself on track, moving toward fulfillment. And watch yourself grow in personal power.

And here is a sentence-completion exercise to further develop the practice of living purposefully:

If I operated 5 percent more purposefully—

If I brought 5 percent more purposefulness to my work—

If I brought 5 percent more purposefulness to my important relationships—

If I brought 5 percent more purposefulness to maintaining good health—

If I want to translate these ideas into action, I will need to—

I am becoming aware—

CHAPTER EIGHT

Integrity

Have you ever had lunch with an old flame, telling your husband you were "with the girls?" Or betrayed a friend's trust because you couldn't resist gossiping? Or falsified your expense account? Or taken credit for an idea not your own? Or buried the achievement of a subordinate because you felt threatened by it? Or remained silent and unprotesting in the face of an evil you knew you should challenge?

Unfortunately, you can read many books on self-esteem today and never learn that behaviors such as these—all of which represent failures of personal integrity—are poison to your sense of self. Self-esteem requires more of you than looking at yourself in the mirror and declaring, "I'm perfect, just as I am."

Unfortunately, women (like men) entertain many fallacious notions about what will nurture self-esteem.

When the strategies don't work, they typically blame themselves but rarely question their underlying assumptions. *If only I say my affirmations every day—if only I do enough community service—if only I find a group of friends to support me with their approval—if only I get this promotion—if only I connect with Mr. Right—then I'll have self-esteem.*

The truth is, some of these attainments might make one happier (although not necessarily), but none generate self-esteem. Self-esteem is a reflection of how we live, how we meet the challenges of life, not what we have, or how we look, or how popular we might be. One of the most important sources of self-esteem is the *integrity* we bring to our daily activities—the congruence between our words and our actions.

When we keep our promises, honor our commitments, deal with others honestly, fairly, and straightforwardly—when we behave in ways we are able to respect—we produce a result far more powerful than the approval of others. *We approve of ourselves.* We feel: I am a person I (and others) can trust; I am proud of my moral choices; I like and admire the kind of person I have made of myself. This is what it means to have self-esteem.

But if, in contrast, our promises and commitments are made on the "expediency" of the moment, with no serious intention of keeping them; if we deal with others dishonestly, manipulatively, and exploitatively; if we behave in ways we are unable to admire—we are left with a result more devastating than others' disapproval. We *disapprove of ourselves.* And the pain of this disapproval cannot be healed in an exercise class or in the bed of a new lover.

Janice, an assistant to an account executive in a brokerage house, wanted to be liked by everyone. She was always making promises to do things for people— more promises than she could possibly keep. She did this on the job and also with her friends. When she failed to keep her promises, she made some people angry—and she thought their anger was the only reason she felt so miserable. It was an act of courage for her slowly to grasp, in therapy, that a deeper source of her distress was the anxious impulsiveness of her promise-making and the recklessness of her promise-breaking.

I gave her a homework assignment to do every day for two weeks—to write six to ten endings for the incomplete sentence, "If I bring a higher level of integrity to my daily activities—."

Her endings included, "I wouldn't make so many promises; I'd keep my word; I wouldn't lie to make people like me; I'd make fewer promises." After experimenting with these policies in action for a month or so, she said, "The thing I'm getting to see so clearly is that, if it's important to me to keep my promises and commitments,

I *really have to be careful about what I agree to do*. I can't always be saying yes to everything and everyone."

In the beginning, it was not easy for her to maintain this policy consistently. But as therapy progressed and her need for others' approval diminished and her self-approval grew, it became natural to say yes when she wanted to say yes and no when she wanted to say no.

"Most of the self-betrayals in my life," she reflected sadly, "had to do with my fear of someone disapproving of me. Now it's my own approval I'm concerned with, not other people's."

Beth was disturbed by the harshness of her husband Tom's disciplining of their two small children. She did not approve of corporal punishment but was frightened that if she challenged Tom's use of it she would place her marriage in jeopardy. Her distress became so acute that she sought therapy. "I feel that I'm betraying my convictions and betraying my children, but mother always taught me a wife's first duty is to go along with her husband. But then, what happens to self-respect?"

I asked, "Would you tell your daughter to treat her personal integrity as less important than not rocking the marriage boat?"

"Certainly not!" she answered indignantly.

Within a week she began to challenge Tom's policy. A while later he agreed to join her in therapy.

Marla was a physician with a practice in the suburbs and an affiliation with a small local hospital. If the combined days her patients spent in the hospital annually passed a certain number, Marla and her husband were rewarded by the hospital with a luxurious cruise. When she knew their insurance was adequate, she often found herself recommending a longer hospital stay for her patients than was strictly necessary. She came to therapy because of mysterious bouts of anxiety and depression. "I've got a wonderful husband—he's a successful dentist—we've got a great home and a great life—I don't know what's the matter with me."

When I learned of her arrangement with the hospital, I inquired how she felt about it and instantly she became defensive. She canceled her next two appointments. When she returned to my office, she complained of a new problem: insomnia. When I reopened the question of her dealings with the hospital, she said angrily, "Well, I suppose I do feel a little guilty, but it's stupid to feel guilty. I mean, who am I really hurting?"

Although symptoms such as hers could have many possible causes, I suspected that the roots of her anxiety, depression, and insomnia all lay in this issue. She was violating her deep sense of right and wrong, and no rationalization could protect her self-esteem. Therapy did not proceed easily. At one point she wondered aloud if perhaps she should drop it and attack her problem with tranquilizers and antidepressants.

The breakthrough occurred when I proposed an experiment. "Would you be willing, for the next two months, to prescribe only hospital stays you're convinced are medically necessary? And let's see what happens." She agreed.

Within ten days her symptoms vanished. At the end of therapy she remarked, "Looking back, I can see that my anxiety and depression were my 'friends.' They were the signals of something wrong in the way I was living. If I had medicated them out of awareness, I would have dug a deeper grave for my self-esteem."

Psychologists do not talk much about integrity. In today's world many people find the word incongruously old-fashioned. It doesn't sound "scientific." I attended a conference once where the subject under discussion was what people do that wounds self-esteem. I was the only one present who brought up the subject of integrity—and breaches of integrity—as relevant. No one else seemed interested in that line of thought. And yet, we do need principles to guide our lives, and the principles we accept had better be reasonable because if we betray them, our self-esteem will suffer. Integrity is one of the guardians of mental health.

A sentence-completion exercise will carry this work further:

If I brought 5 percent more integrity to my daily activities—

If I brought 5 percent more integrity to my work—

If I brought 5 percent more integrity to my relationships—

When I do things I'm not proud of—

If I want to take pride in my choices and actions—

I am beginning to suspect—

I am becoming aware—

PART TWO

Special
Issues

CHAPTER NINE

Romantic Love

Self-esteem is the foundation of romantic love. In its absence, we become saboteurs of our own happiness.

If we feel competent and worthy in our own eyes—if we feel lovable—we have the internal resources (the "emotional wealth") that make it possible for us to love someone else. We are not trapped in feelings of deficiency. We have something to give.

And further, we are able to appreciate others in their own right, as ends in themselves, not merely as instruments for the satisfaction of our needs. So we are able to interact with them appropriately, without exploitativeness or toxic neediness.

But if, in contrast, we do not feel competent and worthy—do not feel lovable—then the basis of our responses to others is a sense of impoverishment—the sense of a deficit. We look for people who will "accept" us, or make the world feel right for us, or rescue us—or else treat us as badly as we feel we deserve to be treated. We are not looking for people to admire, with whom we can share the joy and excitement of life.

If we do not feel lovable, it is very difficult to believe that anyone else loves us. If I cannot accept myself, how can I accept—or believe—your love for me? Your profession of love is confusing, because I know I am not lovable. Your feeling for me cannot possibly be real, reliable, or lasting. It is very difficult to let love in.

I may attempt love, but I am undermined at the base. And in my insecurity I subvert love by demanding excessive reassurances, by venting irrational possessiveness, by making catastrophes of small frictions, by seeking to control through subservience or domination, by finding ways to reject my partner before my partner can reject me. The possibilities for sabotage are unlimited.

As I wrote in *The Psychology of Romantic Love*, "As we see ourselves, so do we act. And our actions tend to produce results that continually support our self-concept" (p. 130).

When I feel deserving of love, I deal with you in a confident, benevolent, and loving manner, and I am open to receive your love. When I feel undeserving of love, I deal with you in a fearful, suspicious, and hostile manner, and you withdraw from me. My self-concept becomes my destiny.

Toni was a successful automobile salesperson, but in her personal life she often caught herself engaging in self-sabotaging behavior. As if to apologize for her success at work, she was oversolicitous with her husband. She was deferential to him when there was no need to be, acting out a conventional notion of "femininity" that he found irritating and bewildering. Trapped by her insecurities, she did not know how to respond when he wondered aloud what had happened to the independent woman he had fallen in love with. In therapy, it took work to help him see how he was reinforcing her "submissive" behavior by making too many decisions that involved them both without consulting her. It took more work to help her overcome the internalized voice of her mother telling her that men do not like strong women. She did not feel confident enough to shrug off her mother's message and relate to her husband without humiliating overcompliance.

Her project became to interact with him as a self-responsible adult—as an independent equal. Success did not come easily. She spoke to me of feeling "naked" without her customary defenses. When her anxiety began to stir in response to fantasies of being abandoned, she learned to "breathe into it," to witness it without being manipulated by it and remain true to her adult self in her behavior—until, over time, she saw that her fears were groundless. In the process, she was doing two things: working on her self-esteem (learning self-assertiveness and authenticity) and protecting her relationship.

Milly, an interior decorator, consciously chose her marriage as an arena in which to work on self-development. She had been very badly hurt in a previous long-term relationship, and now she was terrified of being vulnerable. She longed for her husband's love yet threw up barriers. She blew up small frictions into large conflicts. She fluctuated between not expressing her wants and expressing them with hostility. He reacted with hurt, anger, and withdrawal, which predictably exacerbated her fears. In a counseling session with both of them, I spoke of Masters and Johnson's famous characterization of marriage as "an exchange of vulnerabilities" and of the courage and self-esteem this required.

Working with Milly alone one day, we made a list of the kind of behaviors that would mean she was bringing a higher level of self-esteem to her relationship. She wrote:

I would stay open to what my husband is offering.

I would not engage in self-put-downs.

I would not let anxiety make me withdraw.

I would let my love show.

I would bring benevolence to our encounters.

I would not be sarcastic.

I would not be a nit-picker.

I would express my needs and wants with dignity.

I wouldn't turn every misunderstanding into a catastrophe.

I would listen more.

I would be more generous.

I would not accept unacceptable behavior.

I would allow happiness in my life.

I said to her, "I wonder if these are things you can put into practice now, by choice, without waiting for your self-esteem fully to catch up. Let it be an experiment. Let's discover what would happen if you treat your mate as you know you would treat him if your self-esteem were already where you want it to be."

Of course this was not always easy. Sometimes it was a heroic battle to remain open and loving when the frightened part of her wanted to shut down or run away. Sometimes it was an enormous effort not to attack and vilify when communicating her wants and frustrations. Sometimes she stumbled and fell back on old, counterproductive behaviors. But she did not give up. As she persevered and it got easier, she felt herself becoming stronger and feeling more lovable—and she saw that more of what she wanted in a relationship was coming back to her.

It helped that her husband was also in therapy. But whether we are working on relationship problems alone or with a partner, ultimately what we have to focus on is what is in our volitional control—what we have power over—namely, our own actions. I have often had to work with someone whose partner was not in therapy, and the basic pattern of how to break a vicious cycle of self-sabotaging behavior is the same.

We take the actions we know we would take if we had higher self-esteem. And by taking them we raise our level of self-esteem. And create a life of greater satisfaction.

Is success guaranteed? Will a troubled relationship always be saved? Of course not. But it's the best chance we've got. And one way or the other, we will grow in the process.

CHAPTER TEN

Fear of Selfishness

*Y*ou mean it's not wrong to be selfish?" I have encountered this question in one form or another
throughout all of my professional life, when lecturing or
when doing psychotherapy.

The questioners do not mean, "Do I have permission
to violate the rights of others?," or "Is it appropriate to be
indifferent to human suffering?," or "Are kindness and
generosity not virtues?"

They mean, "Do I have a right to honor my own
needs and wants, to act on my own best judgment, to
strive for my own happiness?" They mean, "Are you
saying I'm not here on earth to live up to anyone else's
expectations?"

I hear some form of this question often when encour-
aging female clients to be more self-assertive in pursuing

their own values. If women feel especially vulnerable to charges of "selfishness," it may be because they are socialized to be caretakers and are given more explicit instructions to think of themselves last.

However, men have their version of the same problem. *Their* burden is the injunction to *perform,* regardless of personal cost, and never, never, never to complain.

I teach enlightened self-interest as a necessity of a rational, fulfilling life, as well as a necessity of self-esteem, and this is an idea about which there is much confusion.

The confusion surrounding this subject is hardly confined to women. From the time we are children, we hear that it is easy to be selfish but that it takes courage to practice self-sacrifice. As anyone who practices psychotherapy knows, it takes courage to do the opposite: to cherish our own desires, to formulate independent values and remain true to them, to fight for our goals whether or not family or friends approve. Giving up what we really want comes all too easily to many people.

When I refer to selfishness in a positive way, I am not speaking of the petty selfishness that consists of recognizing no one's wants but our own or of acting as if others exist only to serve us. I am speaking of the intelligent selfishness of a thinking person who honors her needs and values and is willing to stand up for her legitimate interests.

Rachel was a businesswoman who ran her own print shop and for the past eighteen months had been dating an inordinately self-absorbed surgeon with a limited attention span for any concerns but his own. He made intense speeches about his love for her, but he became annoyed if she interrupted to volunteer a sentence of her own. Charming and gracious in public, he was often moody and demanding when alone with her, due, he explained, to difficulties with a former wife, a troublesome teen-age son, an incompetent office manager, and numerous other people who seemed unwilling to fulfill his expectations.

The result was that with Rachel he found intimacy, physical or emotional, "very stressful." They rarely made love and only at her initiative. He liked to talk about romance but did not actually live a romantic relationship.

When Rachel tried to tell him how hard it was for her sometimes because they never focused on *her* concerns, he interrupted to explain that she did not understand how difficult life was for *him*. Consequently, Rachel tried harder and harder to be sensitive to his suffering while ignoring her own.

After about a month of therapy, she made her first, more assertive effort to convey her frustrations in the relationship. Her lover stopped her dead by hollering, "How can you be so *selfish?!*"

What is significant is not that he said it but that the accusation paralyzed her, causing her to lose all realistic moral perspective. In her mind was the echo of her mother's voice of long ago conveying these thoughts: *Always place others first. Don't say or do anything to make anyone uncomfortable. Selfishness is a sin.* When Rachel heard her lover's accusation of "selfishness," she did not know how to respond.

"Do *you* think I was being selfish?" she asked me.

"Well, you did get tired of always sacrificing your interests to his and you wanted, for once, to have your own feelings respected."

"But is that selfish?" she persisted.

"Sure it is," I answered. "So is breathing."

The point is not that we shouldn't be kind or that it isn't necessary sometimes to defer to the needs of our partner. The point is that a relationship in which one person does the sacrificing while the other does the collecting of sacrificial offerings is immoral and destructive. The purpose of a relationship is joy, not self-annihilation.

Rachel learned to say to him, calmly and factually, "Are you asking me to treat your emotions as more important than mine?" She learned to say, "Are you intending to convey that what you want to say right now is worth hearing but that what I want to say isn't?"

When he finally screamed at her, "Therapy is destroying your femininity!," she knew she had to end the relationship and wondered why she hadn't recognized this sooner, which does not mean it was easy to do.

As women learn to be more self-assertive, they will hear the accusation of "selfishness" more often. The accusation is commonly used as a tool of manipulation and control. Disarmed by guilt, people often relinquish their own interests, as the accuser demands.

When a client of mine, Astrid, a sculptor, informed her parents that she had decided not to have children but instead to invest all her energies in her career, they demanded, "How can you be so selfish?"

When Florence, a real-estate broker, announced her plans to remarry, her eighteen-year-old son reproached her. "Now you won't have so much time for me. How can you be so selfish?"

When Maxine, a paralegal who had helped put her husband through school asked for his help in financing her education now that he was established professionally, he responded, "Why have you turned selfish and demanding?"

When Mallory, the co-owner of a gourmet food shop, explained to her business partner that their relationship was not working, that she felt overburdened and exploited because the partner was not carrying her fair share of the load, and that she had decided to start a new business on her own, her partner protested, "God, you've become so *selfish*! I thought we were *friends*."

As to women and men who are selfish in the petty sense and who have no interest in anyone's needs but their own while expecting others to cater to them, what they need to learn is not self-sacrifice but justice and objectivity. The problem with such people is not that they are selfish but that they have a fool's (or a child's) notion of self-interest.

However, today's women are beginning to wake up. Imagine the response if a lecturer told a group of modern women, "Don't think of your own needs and wants—think only of the needs and wants of those you serve. Self-sacrifice is your highest virtue." But men need to think about this issue, too. It affects everyone.

Until we understand that each human being is an end in him- or herself, not a means to the ends of others, we cannot treat ourselves or others decently. Until we understand that we are no one's property, just as no one is our property—and that we must deal with one another as independent, self-responsible equals, not sacrificial objects—then all we can argue about is who gets to collect. What we will *not* have is self-esteem.

Not a good basis for a life. Not a good basis for relationships either.

CHAPTER ELEVEN

Jealousy

I am often asked whether jealousy is always an indication of poor self-esteem or whether high-self-esteem people ever experience this painful emotion.

The short answer is that more often than not, jealousy *is* a reflection of inadequate self-esteem—*but not always or necessarily*. There are circumstances in which jealousy can be felt by women and men who are relatively free of self-doubt.

Passionate love—romantic love—entails a desire for sexual exclusivity. Consequently, some degree of pain follows the loss of that exclusivity, as when one's partner has a sexual encounter with someone else. If one wants to call that pain jealousy, then I would say it is normal and would not draw any inferences about the self-esteem of the sufferer.

If, however, the sufferer felt not merely pain but devastated self-worth, then I would say that she or he had a self-esteem problem and that it existed prior to the infidelity. "If he could betray me by sleeping with *her*," said Jan, owner of a cleaning establishment, "then what value do I have? He's reduced my self-esteem to zero." The problem was not that Jan felt pain; in the circumstances, that was normal. The problem lay in the conclusion she drew about herself.

No person whose self-esteem is solid in the first place imagines that another person, over whose actions one has no control, can destroy it. The only person's actions we are responsible for are our own. No one else's behavior can be a reflection on our worth (if we do not sanction or support that behavior). That was the lesson Jan needed to learn.

Jealousy generally involves anxiety, feelings of being threatened, pain, fantasies of rejection or abandonment, and often rage in response to our partner's (real or imagined) involvement with another.

Some people feel jealousy because they experience deep self-doubt and live with the constant anticipation of rejection and abandonment. But there are a number of other situations (besides infidelity) that can provoke jealousy in people both with and without self-confidence. Jealousy can arise from a generalized apprehension that somehow love and happiness always die. Some people experience jealousy when they see someone else receiving the interest or kindness they want themselves. Some feel it when they see their partner flirting. And jealousy may arise in a new relationship because of painful experiences in past relationships involving a partner's infidelities.

Clearly, the more self-confident we are and the more we trust and feel loved by our partner, the less likely we are to experience jealousy in its extreme forms. We can have occasional feelings of jealousy without being "a jealous person."

If we ask, "Does romantic love inevitably entail some feelings of pain or fear at the prospect of loss, even among self-confident individuals?"—then the answer is yes. But if we ask, "Is anxiety, pain, or rage over potential rivals an inevitable part of love for everyone?"—then I would answer no.

But suppose we *do* feel insecure and *are* inclined to jealousy. What can we do to manage such feelings so as not to destroy our relationship?

When we're jealous, we often respond by becoming depressed and withdrawn, which leaves our partner feeling uncomfortable and rejected. Another common response is anger, which tends to provoke defensiveness and hostility. Both reactions exacerbate an already difficult situation and make communication almost impossible.

So we need to learn alternative responses that are more helpful.

When Clara, a legal secretary, saw her husband flirting with another woman at a party, she instantly became hostile and bitter; her husband denied everything, and for several days they barely spoke. In therapy she learned to say, when she saw it happening, "Watching you, I felt a little anxious; I felt a little scared. I began having fantasies of your running off and leaving me." She took responsibility for her own feelings and did what she could to create a context in which a benevolent discussion could take place. She did not disown her anger, recognizing that it was understandable in the circumstances, but saw that her interests were not served by making anger the heart of her communication. Because he did not feel attacked, her husband did not try to defend himself. He listened. He acknowledged that he had been flirting and that he had been unintentionally hurtful. The problem was not solved in that instant, but the road was opened for a deeper, more meaningful exploration.

We need to recognize our feelings, own them, talk about them honestly, and not allow them to drive us to behavior that sabotages relationships.

This is equally true when our initial response is to withdraw into hurt silence. The only hope of a solution lies in authentic, nonaccusatory communication and an honest sharing of feelings.

Lauren, a stockbroker, complained of feeling jealous because of the attention other women paid to her handsome husband. She insisted that he must be inviting it by somehow signaling availability. When I asked her what she would like her husband to do differently, she could not answer. I encouraged her to talk about her anxieties with him rather than withdraw into depressed silence. In their conversations it slowly emerged that he did enjoy being the center of so much feminine attention and that, if he did nothing to encourage it, he did nothing to discourage it either. After some resistance, he agreed to be more reserved. She agreed to take responsibility for her fears, monitor them, talk about them—and keep reminding herself that her husband was not the father who had left his family for another woman when Lauren was twelve.

If we are the person doing the flirting and our partner is the jealous one, our first responsibility is to be truthful. If we deny our partner's perceptions, we merely deepen their anxiety and confirm their fear that there is something to be jealous about.

"When Bob would call me on my flirting," said Linda, an editor, "my first impulse was to say it was only his imagination. I had to learn not to be controlled by my fear of being reproached; it made me deny what was obviously true. I didn't have a lot of dates when I was young, and sometimes male attention goes to my head.

When I admitted that to Bob, he got more relaxed; he said he could understand that. His understanding made me want to handle my feelings better, experience them without being run by them, not act inappropriately or do anything that could give him grounds for discomfort."

Jealously, justified or not, is painful—and humiliating. It needs to be dealt with compassionately, whether in ourselves or our partner. When we have the courage to explore the pain and fear that underlie it, it tends to diminish—as self-esteem tends to grow.

CHAPTER TWELVE

Expressing Anger

The problem for some of us is that when we are angry, we say terrible things we later regret. The problem for others is that they do not communicate their feelings at all.

Anger is often a troublesome and confusing emotion. Unfortunately, when we were growing up, no one ever told us how to handle it. Often, the implication was that if we were a good person we would never experience it, let alone express it.

And yet all of us have moments of anger. No matter how much we care for them, sometimes we get angry with our partner, our children, our friends.

The commonest mistake we make when we are angry is to engage in personal attacks, moralizing, and psychologizing. "Only a rotten neurotic behaves this way!

You're just like our mother, who's the most screwed-up individual I've ever met! You're really disgusting!" All such communications are aimed at the listener's self-esteem; what they accomplish is to invite defensiveness and counterattack.

Do you want the other person's mind engaged in trying to understand your point or in trying to defend him- or herself? Character assassination always leads the person's mind away from the key issue and toward self-protection and self-justification. If your primary motive is to inflict pain, character assassination is a good way to do it. But if your goal is mutual understanding and resolution, it's self-defeating.

What, then, is an appropriate way to express anger? I suggest the following steps:

Describe, factually, the action or event to which you are responding so that the listener knows exactly what triggered your anger. Sometimes people sound off for ten minutes before the other party even knows what the source of the upset is. Say something like, "Often you make belittling remarks when I disagree with what you say . . . "

Describe your feelings. Say something like, ". . . and that leaves me feeling indignant and offended."

Describe what you want done. Say something like, "If you think I'm mistaken when I disagree with you, answer my arguments. Don't resort to sarcasm and personal abuse."

If you are able to be calm, fine, but you are under no obligation to speak in a pleasant tone of voice. You have a right to your anger. My concern here is with the *content* of what you say.

Here is an example of what effective communication might sound like: "It's taken me a long time to learn to speak honestly with you about things that bother me, and it isn't always easy for me, even now. When I talk to you, you listen without responding, and nothing seems to change in your behavior. I feel frustrated, helpless, invisible, and angry. It would mean a great deal to me if, after you've heard what I have to say, you would share with me your thoughts and feelings about it."

The listener will find it easier to hear and respond appropriately because there are neither accusations nor attacks nor threats.

In extreme situations, there's nothing wrong with saying, "I need some time out. I'm too angry. I don't trust myself to speak right now."

In contrast to those who express anger in ways that are destructive, there are those who suffer in silence, feeling, "Who am I to protest? Who am I to stick up for myself?"

Louise, married and doing volunteer work at a local hospital, once complained, "Whenever my mother-in-law comes to visit, she talks only to her son, acts as if I'm not present." She said that she was frightened to convey her anger at this. I asked her what she might say if she were not frightened. "I would tell her . . . " she groped for words helplessly. "I would tell her, 'You're so mean; you're really inconsiderate; you're really a rotten, contemptible person. . . . '"

I asked her to consider how it would feel to say, instead, "I would like to look forward to your visits here. But when I see that you talk only to your son and ignore me as if I were not here, I find it impossible to enjoy your presence or look forward to your coming."

She answered instantly, "Oh, that would be much more frightening!"

When I pointed out that I neither shouted nor said anything abusive, she replied, "Yes, but in my version, with all the insults, the focus is on *her.* I'm not talking about myself. That's safer. In your version, the focus is on me, on my feelings. To say what you said, *I'd have to act as if my feelings counted.*"

Precisely. One of the ways that self-esteem expresses itself is in respecting our own feelings, needs, and dignity— treating ourselves as valuable. Those with poor self-esteem can fear this self-assertiveness. But the fear can be overcome.

We need to learn to practice what the late child psychologist Haim Ginott called "anger without insult." It does not come naturally. Learning it takes discipline. For some of us, like Louise, the discipline will consist of learning to speak up at all. For others, it will consist of learning to convey a protest without using words aimed at inflicting humiliation and pain.

While learning the art of anger without insult, it is useful to ask ourselves, "Is my purpose to hurt and humiliate or to inspire understanding and evoke change?" or "Is my purpose to have a catharsis or to communicate constructively?"

It is important to be able to speak up when we feel we are being treated badly or when our values are under attack. What we need to master is not the suppression of all feelings of anger or protest but the art of constructive communication—meaning communication that produces desirable results.

To be sure, there will be occasions when we may decide that in this moment it does not serve our purposes to express anger. But at such times as we do express it, let us do so in a way that will give us the best chance of being heard and responded to appropriately. One day this basic skill will be taught to school children.

CHAPTER THIRTEEN

Defensiveness

Sometimes we try to protect our self-esteem in ways that hurt it. Our intention is to take care of ourselves, but we achieve the opposite—and leave a bad taste in the soul. A prime example of such behavior is *defensiveness*.

Someone asks us a question, challenges us in some way, or criticizes something we have done. To stave off painful feelings that erupt within us, such as embarrassment or anxiety, we respond by alienating, rationalizing, counterattacking, or otherwise avoiding the issue that has been raised. We react *defensively*. In such cases our primary concern is not, What is the truth of this situation? but rather, How can I spare myself discomfort?

When we respond this way, self-esteem suffers, because what we are ultimately avoiding are facts of reality.

There is an intimate relationship between self-esteem and a respect for facts. Women and men of healthy self-esteem do not make themselves adversaries of truth. Rather, their strength lies in the knowledge that their aim is always to ally themselves with what *is*—with reality— as best they are given to understand it. They operate mindfully, responsibly, and authentically. This is the secret of their power.

But when our self-esteem is shaky, we may come to identify it not with our rationality but with our ability to dissolve discomfiting facts in mental fog, that is, with the success of our defensive tactics.

Thus we drive deeper the fear that if our behavior were exposed to full daylight, our self-esteem (or our pretense at it) could not survive. We drive deeper the poisonous idea that reality is the enemy to be kept at bay. No blow delivered by anyone else could be more hurtful to our sense of self than the blow we deliver through this practice.

Gwen worked for a firm that produced consumer electronic equipment. She came to my office, angry, after a row with her manager, Nora. It took me a long time to find out that the explosion was precipitated by Nora asking Gwen one question: "Why did you tell our customer that we would deliver his order Friday when you know we can't possibly deliver it earlier than next Wednesday?" The question was asked in a normal, nonaccusatory tone of voice (as Gwen later acknowledged). In response, Gwen hollered, "Would you ask me that question if I were a *man*?" The implication was that Nora would tolerate lying in a man but not in a woman, which the supervisor did not appreciate—and answered with considerable heat of her own.

"So, tell me," I said to Gwen, "why *did* you lie to your customer?" After considerable dancing around, she finally answered, "Because I was afraid of his anger if I told him the truth."

I then asked Gwen to say aloud, three times, "I lied to our customer about the delivery date because I was afraid of his anger." By means of this simple exercise, I wanted her to fully own and experience what she was telling me. When she had done so, I asked her how she felt, and with a deep sigh she replied, "Cleaner."

I suggested that therapy could help her grow out of her fear of anger but that, in the meantime, it was better to face the fear than the consequences of surrendering to it. She said, "When the order doesn't arrive, I'm *really* going to face anger." I inquired how she felt about telling Nora, her supervisor, what she had identified. After some stumbling and elusiveness, Gwen answered, "Scared. But I'll do it. I owe her that."

I asked what would have been painful about telling Nora the truth in the first place, and she replied, "I would have had to confront the embarrassing and humiliating fact of my fear of anger." Thus does self-protection turn into self-sabotage.

Charlene and Alex came to me for marriage counseling. She was a freelance copywriter; he worked in the production department of an advertising firm. Married for seventeen years, they had two teenage sons; most of their fights were about the boys' upbringing.

Her complaint was that Alex had no confidence in her judgment as a mother and no appreciation of how much responsibility she carried. "He can't understand why I'm tired and sometimes irritable," she said angrily. "He gets upset when I shriek or yell at the boys—as if I don't have provocation."

His complaint was that, no matter what care he took in choosing his words so as not to give offense or cause pain, she interpreted any suggestion or observation of his as a personal attack, to which she responded with indignation and counterattack.

"I never impugn her competence or her motives," Alex said. "I never disparage her worth. But if I suggest that talking to our sons calmly, respectfully, and firmly works better than insults and ridicule, she becomes enraged and says that I don't appreciate what she does and that I always assume my judgment is superior to hers."

It was clear that, whatever the reasons, Charlene did not feel her contributions were appreciated or that her husband truly regarded her as his intellectual equal. "Because I'm a woman," she said bitterly. I agreed that some men are condescending and disrespectful to their wives. Then I asked how Alex conveyed the negative messages she felt she was hearing. She was unable to tell me. I said that I saw no trace of that attitude on his part in their exchanges in my office.

"*All* men are that way," she retorted. "God knows my father was." She spoke of the contempt with which her father had treated her mother, and her mother's submissive compliance. "I swore no man would treat me that way."

I asked if it was possible that, based on her childhood experiences, she already expected the worst from Alex even before he said a word. I wondered aloud if that might be the root of her agitation when he challenged any of her interactions with their children.

"Damn right," she said, after a long moment's thought. "I walk around feeling defensive."

"When you were a young girl," I said, "it must have been very painful . . . seeing your father's behavior toward your mother."

"Not just toward my mother," she answered sharply. "Toward me as well. Toward any female."

"When I speak," said Alex, "I'd like you to see and hear *me*. Me the individual. Not some imaginary reincarnation of your father. Otherwise, I feel like the invisible man. Women say they want to be seen as persons, not as stereotypes. So do men."

Defensiveness

Charlene had no difficulty agreeing in principle, but the day-by-day implementation was not learned easily. Her defensiveness felt like a survival strategy, without which she could be annihilated.

Wanting Alex to understand this, I said to him, "In a raging sea, one does not throw away a lifebelt."

To Charlene I said, "What I'm hoping you'll come to grasp is that your life is not a raging sea and that your defensiveness isn't saving you. It's drowning you."

"What's the way out?" She asked.

"Well, to begin with, when someone says something to you, it's helpful if your first priority is to hear and understand what they've said. Sounds simple, doesn't it? But, you know, for many people that's the hardest part. Learning it takes a lot of discipline."

Sometimes we can be defensive even when we know we have done nothing wrong, and the other person's criticism, suggestions, or challenges rest on mistaken assumptions. As soon as we hear anything that can be construed, rightly or wrong, as a challenge to our behavior, we drop into a defend-and-attack mode—in other words, we drop into a *this-is-war* mentality.

This attitude is often expressed by people who were subjected to a great deal of criticism and chastisement as youngsters, whether from parents, teachers, or other authority figures. They grew up hearing themselves rebuked so many times that they became "gun-shy" and hyper-reactive at the first hint, real or imagined, of a criticism. Such persons can be extraordinarily difficult to deal with, even though they may have many other attractive traits and virtues. One feels that with them, there cannot be the normal give-and-take of honest feedback.

Lucille was a research psychologist whose mother had been a high school principal and whose father had been a highly respected surgeon. Both parents were brilliant, highly intellectual, and judgmental to an extreme degree. Lucille felt that every time she turned around, one parent or the other found something to rebuke her for, sometimes with cruelly hurtful sarcasm. She recalled tensing her body every time she came home from school, anticipating an attack. To defend herself, she learned to lie, to live as much of her life in secret as she could, and, above all, to alibi.

At the university where she worked, the same pattern continued. If anyone raised a question about any aspect of her work, she instantly translated what was said into an attack and shifted into high defensiveness. When her work was praised, as it often was, she barely heard what was said; it did not register; she was not "programmed" for praise, only for criticism, which she often heard when none was intended. If and when someone did question and perhaps criticize something she had done, she responded by taking the conversation off in some irrelevant direction, blaming someone else, or challenging the speaker's knowledge or motives. This did not make her popular with her colleagues. She came to me in panic because she was afraid her reputation would cause her not to get tenure.

In therapy, after exploring the childhood roots of her problem, we focused on breaking down the sequence that began with someone else's comment and ended with her defensive reaction and, often, counterattack.

The first link in the chain was hearing some statement that she interpreted, not necessarily correctly, as a criticism. The next link, a microsecond later, was the thought, *I am being attacked.* In the next microsecond she felt anxiety—the third link. The fourth was her effort to subdue her anxiety by saying the first thing that flashed into her mind, which was usually something inappropriate.

We noted that as the confrontation continued, she typically heard less and less of what the other person was actually saying, because her mind was filled with imaginings of what the other person *really meant* (such as that she was stupid or incompetent or a bad human being).

This is a pattern one often encounters. When people are defensive, their perceptions tend to be highly distorted. Consequently, their responses are not appropriate. They answer what has *not* been said, while failing to answer what has been said.

In helping Gwen, Charlene, and Lucille, as well as many other people, to overcome their defensiveness, I have found it useful to focus on some very specific steps. These can be practiced by anyone who relates to the problem I am describing.

Train yourself to focus on hearing what is literally being said. Take a moment to replay the exact statement in your mind.

Consciously breathe slowly and deeply so that you do not become uncontrollably tense and so that anxiety does not take over and dictate your responses.

Answer what has been said as precisely and accurately as you can. If you need time to think, or are confused, say so. But stay with the facts. Do not go into irrelevancies and, above all, do not counterattack.

After you have answered what has been said literally and truthfully, if you feel there is additional information you need to impart in order to make your actions more understandable, convey this as a separate and distinct thought. Do not blend this into your initial response.

Accept that if you have a history of defensiveness, these steps will almost inevitably evoke some anxiety in you. *Tolerate the anxiety.* Observe it, go on breathing slowly and deeply, *and do not let yourself be manipulated by it.* For some of us, this will be a hard discipline to learn, but it *can* be learned and the rewards are enormous.

The first reward is cleaner and more successful communications. The second is that you will gain a reputation for honesty and integrity.

CHAPTER FOURTEEN

Success Anxiety

Self-esteem energizes us in the pursuit of our goals. It allows us to feel satisfaction and comfort with our successes. When our self-esteem is solid, success feels natural and appropriate to us.

However, when self-esteem is weak, success can trigger anxiety—and anxiety can trigger self-sabotaging behavior. Today, when more and more women are entering the workplace, many of them starting their own businesses, I encounter some version of this problem with considerable frequency.

I call the problem "success anxiety." It is the dread and disorientation that persons of inadequate self-esteem experience when career or work-life go well in ways that conflict with their deepest vision of who they are and what is appropriate to them.

"I've always been energetic and ambitious," said Jan, owner of a small chain of boutiques. "When I married David, a medical technician, who's much less of a go-getter than I am, I told myself I didn't care about the differences between us because he was a warm, sensitive person and that was what mattered. But when my business became successful, I started to feel guilty toward David, because I was making so much more than he was. I was also angry at him for not being motivated. There was this voice inside my head saying, 'Women aren't supposed to do this well; they're not supposed to surpass their husbands.' I became so filled with guilt and anger that I began to fight with important clients—and the business began to go downhill. Now, three years and a lot of nightmares later, I'm trying to build the business up again. But I need to know what went wrong and why, so that when I succeed, I won't repeat the same pattern."

"The more money I make," said Eleanor, an attorney, "the harder it is for me to sleep without pills. I keep feeling something is wrong, something doesn't fit, this isn't supposed to be happening."

"Every time I get a real break," said Toni, a struggling actress, "I do something stupid to screw it up. Be late. Keep forgetting my lines. Be rude to the star. Fight with the director. All I dream about is making it in my work—and the prospect of succeeding terrifies me."

"'Where'd you get the idea you were supposed to be happy?' my mother used to say to me," remarked Michelle, a buyer in a large department store. "I can still hear her snapping, 'You're no brain-truster and you're no world-beater, either.' Three times I was up for a major promotion, and three times I did something to wreck it. Once could have been an accident, but three times? No. I'm doing it myself. If I didn't, my fear would go through the roof. The thought of being successful in spite of Mother's predictions and without Mother's blessing scares me. It's like being flung out into the void."

Sometimes fear of success is the disguised form of what is really fear of failure—fear that we will be unable to sustain our achievements. But not necessarily. We may experience genuine fear of success if we feel unworthy or undeserving of it, or associate it with abandonment and loss of love (of mother, father, husband, whomever).

When we feel anxious it is natural to look for ways to reduce our anxiety. We may take a pill, jog, overeat, have sex, go shopping, take a drink—or seek to eliminate the immediate cause of the anxiety. If success makes us anxious, we may seek to reduce the success to a lower, more tolerable level. We may sabotage our efforts to achieve our professed goals.

This process is not usually conscious. A woman may insist, "Of course I'm entitled to be successful! Look how hard I work!" At the conscious level, this statement may be sincere. And yet, at a deeper level, when self-esteem is weak, success can evoke apprehension and disorientation. There is the wordless sense, "This is not the way my life is supposed to be." One feels temporarily out of sync with reality. And that is necessarily frightening. One feels, "This is a mistake. It can't last. I'll be found out or exposed. Or something else will go wrong."

Self-esteem is the experience of being competent to cope with the basic challenges of life *and of being worthy of happiness* (which includes being worthy of success). To feel "worthy of happiness" is to feel that self-fulfillment is natural and appropriate, not an aberration of the natural order that will vanish at any moment.

Not everyone who has a self-esteem problem has it to the same extent, and not everyone who suffers success anxiety does so equally. Like everything else in human psychology, it is a matter of degree. You may be aware that success ignites some measure of discomfort in you, yet you are not driven to drastic self-sabotage. You may not undercut yourself completely; you may only retard your progress, holding yourself down to a lower level of achievement than is possible, while wondering about the mysterious barrier you cannot seem to crash through, oblivious to the fact that the source of your frustration lies within.

The truth is, you are entitled to any success you are able to earn by your honest effort. But it may take enormous courage to accept this. When we see ourselves moving toward success and anxiety kicks in, we must learn *to do nothing*, that is, to keep out of our own way. We must learn to breathe into our feelings, to allow them, to watch our own process, to enter into the depths of the experience while at the same time being a conscious witness to it, *and not be manipulated by anxiety into behaving self-destructively.* Then, in time, we can build a tolerance for success. We can increase our ability to handle it without panicking.

We must learn to recognize anxiety when it arises. We must learn to identify the ways in which we tend to self-sabotage *so that we can make a conscious effort to abstain from doing those things.*

By way of facilitating this learning, I sometimes ask my psychotherapy clients to write six to ten endings every day for a few weeks to these incomplete sentences:

At the thought of becoming more successful, I—

I get anxious at work when—

One of the ways I self-sabotage in my
work is—

One of the ways I obstruct my progress in my
work is—

If I can allow myself to be successful today—

Slowly, in this manner, they discover that a new way of being is possible. Success gradually loses its terror. But without courage, the process cannot begin; without perseverance, it cannot be completed. Joy may be our birthright, but it cannot be claimed without effort.

PART THREE

Empowering Strategies

CHAPTER FIFTEEN

Trying Something Different

One of the pleasures in being a psychotherapist is that I sometimes have the opportunity to experiment with mildly mischievous solutions to clients' difficulties.

Nadine was a mother and office manager who worked on personal problems with me via the telephone. My office is in Los Angeles, and her home is in Minneapolis. This afternoon she sounded desperate.

"God, I wish you were a woman today!" were her first words. "I don't know if a man will have sympathy for this problem."

She presented the following dilemma. Her husband was a research scientist who had his own laboratory; she ran his office in addition to running his home and raising their two teenage boys. She made only one request of them: when she entered her kitchen to make dinner, she wanted to find the garbage pail empty and all dirty dishes in the dishwater. Her husband and sons agreed to take turns discharging this responsibility, but they rarely followed through. Before she began to cook, she usually had to clean up the kitchen, which she bitterly resented. The men in her family agreed that she was absolutely right . . . only nothing ever changed.

"I've reasoned with them," Nadine said. "I've pleaded, I've screamed, I've begged. Nothing works. I feel utterly ineffectual. What should I do?"

"Are you absolutely committed to getting a change?" I asked.

"I'd do *anything*," she declared.

"Good. I think you can help these gentlemen to keep their promises if you'll do exactly as I say."

Next evening, when she found the kitchen dirty, she walked into the living room and began reading a book. When her puzzled husband and sons inquired about dinner, she answered, smiling pleasantly, "I don't cook in a dirty kitchen." (I had told her, "No reproaches and no explanations.") The men exchanged disoriented looks and disappeared into the kitchen. A few minutes later, when they informed her it was now spotless, she proceeded—cheerfully—to prepare their dinner.

The next night the kitchen was clean when she first entered it.

The night after that, the garbage pail was full again and there were dirty dishes on the counter. (I had told her this was likely.) Without saying a word, she exited and resumed her reading. Soon she heard them reproaching one another for not cleaning up and negotiating who would be responsible for what. (I had told her, when that happened, to stay out of it. "It's not your problem. All you have to know is that you don't cook in a dirty kitchen.")

For several weeks, she always entered a clean kitchen at dinnertime. I had warned her to be prepared for at least one more "test." But when once again she found the kitchen dirty, she was tempted to overlook it because of their recent efforts. I had cautioned her that this was the moment at which the experiment would succeed or fail, depending on the consistency of her response. So she summoned all her will power and went back to her book.

That ended the problem. What she had not accomplished with words, she accomplished with actions.

I said to her, "If something doesn't work, don't keep doing it. You need to *change your behavior* in order to compel them to change *theirs*. You gave them a strong reason to cooperate with you and to do what they had promised to do. The moral of the story is, when you hit a wall, look for new actions to take.

Della, a newspaper journalist, was unhappy because of her lover's disposition to make belittling cracks at her expense. She said, "The crazy thing is, Mel is a kind, good-natured man most of the time. But that sarcasm is something he heard his father do, and he just naturally falls into it whenever he's frustrated. He apologizes later, but just the same, it hurts. Nothing I say to him makes a difference. He won't go to therapy. I don't know what to do. Should I just put up with it because of all his virtues?"

"I think we can do better than that," I answered.

The next time he made a sarcastic remark, she reached for her bag, pulled out a notebook, glanced at her watch, and began to write.

"What are you doing?" he asked, bewildered and a little impatient.

As instructed, she smiled warmly and replied, "Our relationship is so very important to me, and sometimes you say things that are really memorable and I want to have a record of them." ("Remember," I had told her, "no rebukes.")

On another occasion, she said benevolently, "Would you mind repeating that? I'd like to get your words down exactly. Your thoughts are so important to me."

At first he'd apologize, or laugh, or say, "Branden is putting you up to this, isn't he?" But, as advised, she refused to be drawn into a discussion of what she was doing. She did not become angry, she did not explain herself, and she did not debate. (This had taken more than a little coaching.)

In the second week, there were no incidents.

In the third week, he slipped twice and when she began to write he got a little angry, but she pleasantly refused to be drawn into an argument.

In the third and forth weeks, there were no incidents.

In the fifth week, he began a sarcastic remark once, stopped himself, and apologized.

"What exactly have I done?" Della demanded of me.

"Most of the unkind things people say, they wouldn't say if in the moment they were fully conscious of what they were doing. Mel's got a very bad habit he needs to break. All you're doing is raising his awareness in the moment of action."

In the sixth week, Mel phoned me to discuss entering therapy.

No general formula can provide the right response for all situations. My hope is that these stories may inspire creative responses of your own, when rational conversation gets you nowhere. If a particular strategy fails, *try something different.* Remember Einstein's definition of insanity: doing the same thing over and over again, but expecting a different result.

CHAPTER SIXTEEN

Knowing Our Boundaries

Irene, a stockbroker, came to therapy because she was overwhelmed by guilt following the suicide of her closest woman friend. She had begged her depressed friend to seek professional help, but her friend had refused. She had spent hundreds of hours trying to help her friend out of her pain, to no avail. "If only I had found a way to stop her," she cried to me in therapy. "If only I had given her hope somehow."

In working through this problem, we saw that she identified too much of her feelings of worth with being a "helper." Unconsciously, she imagined that she was—or should be—all-powerful. When her friend swallowed a bottle of sleeping pills, Irene's self-esteem collapsed; or rather, her illusion of self-esteem collapsed, as self-esteem based on fantasy and self-delusion is not real in the first place.

Irene had always prided herself on her sense of responsibility. If there was a problem, whether it was hers or someone else's, she took it upon herself to solve it. She enjoyed her feelings of competence, and she enjoyed the appreciation she received. She had very little experience of defeat, and when it came—in the form of her friend's suicide—she was devastated.

A sense of responsibility is a virtue. But to practice it intelligently, we need to understand that we can only be responsible in matters open to our choice. We need to know what is within our power and also what is not within our power. Otherwise, misguided notions of "responsibility" can be calamitous for us.

The truth is, we are responsible for our own choices and actions and for no one else's. We may be able to influence but we cannot control another mind. We cannot determine what someone else will think or do. We need to learn where our boundaries are. This is what Irene had to come to grips with in therapy.

As a child, she had seen her mother fulfill the role of the inexhaustible caregiver, not only with the immediate family but also with relatives and friends. She saw that if someone was in trouble, her mother immediately "merged" with that individual and took responsibility for finding a solution—and felt unhappy when she couldn't. In therapy Irene remarked, "I grew up thinking that being a woman *meant* not having boundaries."

Florence was an office manager in a cosmetics business. Her staff often came to her with problems it was their task to solve. Florence found it difficult to say no to anyone and spent long hours after quitting time doing the work of other people. When I pointed out that she was not discharging the duties for which she had been hired—namely, inspiring other people to solve their problems rather than giving them ready-made solutions—she answered, "You're right, of course, but why do I find it so difficult to refuse when people ask for help? I have a terror of being thought selfish. I hear our minister's voice, saying, 'Woman, be a giver, not a taker.'"

"How about," I asked, "being a woman who carries her own weight and requires others to do likewise?"

"Do you think that would be feminine?" she inquired hesitantly.

In their socialization women are often encouraged to identify themselves as caretakers who recognize no boundaries between themselves and others. To challenge this notion may require independence and courage. It may require saying no to the internalized voices of authority figures from one's childhood.

I gave Florence a sentence-completion exercise in the hope of clarifying this issue. I gave her the sentence stem, "If I would say no when I want to say no and yes when I want to say yes—," and asked her to keep repeating this stem, putting a different ending on it each time. Here is what she said:

"If I would say no when I want to say no and yes when I want to say yes—I'd be a different person; people might not like me; I'd get more done; I'd take better care of myself; I'd have more self-respect; my staff would have to grow up; I'd stop treating them as children; I'd learn intelligent self-responsibility and I'd teach it to the people I supervise."

Sometimes people take on inappropriate responsibility for others as a way of avoiding taking proper responsibility for themselves. Unconsciously, they seek to lose themselves in the problems of others. When women are told, in effect, that femininity equals "selflessness," they are encouraged down this road. If independence and self-responsibility feel like a burden, this doctrine can be seductive.

However, misguided notions of responsibility are not a monopoly of women. Sometimes parents—fathers as much as mothers—torture themselves because, even though they have done their honest, conscientious best, their children do not develop as the parents had hoped—and the parents feel guilt. They imagine themselves to possess a power no human being possesses: the power to determine what choices another person will make. If children need to learn where they end and their parents begin, parents need to learn the same lesson.

Sometimes a wife despairs because in spite of her best efforts, she cannot stop her husband's drinking. Sometimes a husband despairs because no matter what he does he cannot stop his wife's attachment to tranquilizers. If only I knew the right thing to say or do, they may tell themselves—as if total power could be theirs if they could just tap into it. They may believe in their own free will, but they do not believe in their partner's. They do not accept the boundaries that separate one human being from another.

One of the meanings of living responsibly is knowing what we are and are not responsible for. We need to know what is and is not subject to our volitional choice—what is and is not within our power—what is up to us and what isn't. Without this understanding, we cannot practice intelligent self-responsibility, and we cannot protect ourselves against others' inappropriate demands—or the inappropriate demands we place upon ourselves.

CHAPTER SEVENTEEN

Building a Career

The phone call was from Boston, and as soon as I heard Theodora's voice I knew that she was angry. Although my office is in Los Angeles, I have a number of clients in other cities who, like Theodora, consult with me via the telephone. "Life is really unfair!" were her first words after we said hello.

Theodora worked for a company that manufactured computer parts and dreamed of a career in the computer industry. When I asked her what was upsetting her today, she spoke about the chaos in her office, the inefficient filing system, the unnecessary duplication of effort, and a plan she had developed six months ago for a radical overhaul of the office system that would have resulted in greater convenience and efficiency. Her words tumbled out with rising agitation.

"So what's the problem?" I asked.

The problem, she declared, was that a coworker had submitted a proposal similar to her idea, had gained the support of many associates in advance of taking the idea to their boss, had won approval to have the plan implemented, and was now being rewarded with a raise and a promotion. "She beat me to it!" Theodora protested. "The promotion should have been mine!"

When I asked if she meant that her coworker had stolen her idea, Theodora answered, "No. I never told anyone about it. But it was *my* idea. Life is so unfair."

"Theodora," I said gently, *"everyone* has some good ideas from time to time. What distinguishes the winners is that they *do something* with their ideas. Look at what your coworker did. She got a valuable idea, tested it out in conversations with associates, gained their support, then took it to her boss—and, I would guess, was probably well prepared to answer any questions or objections the boss might raise. *That's* why she succeeded. *That's* what made the difference."

There was a long moment of silence.

Then she said in a sad, muted voice, "I guess it's idiotic to expect to be recognized for an idea I hadn't told anybody about."

What intrigued me was why she had kept the plan to herself for so long, without communicating it to anyone. I knew that this was not an uncommon problem.

People often have excellent ideas that they consign to the impotence of daydreams—never taking action in reality to see them realized and implemented.

One woman might be more intelligent than another and have more creative ideas, yet be far less successful because the second woman takes her own ideas more seriously; she nurtures them, develops them, and fights for their acceptance in the workplace. The difference lies not in brainpower but in drive and motivation—in *commitment*.

Theodora whispered, "I think some part of me felt, if this idea is really so good, how come no one else has thought of it?"

I asked if she understood Groucho Marx's joke that he would not belong to any club that would have him as a member.

Another long pause. Then she said, "You mean, if the idea occurred to me—how good could it be? That kind of attitude?"

"Well, that is a possibility. What do you think?"

"I never expect to be listened to. I never expect to be taken seriously."

"Sounds like you don't listen to yourself. Sounds like you don't take yourself seriously. You discount your own ideas because they're yours. Then you get hurt and angry when other people don't treat you better than you treat yourself."

When we doubt our minds, we tend to discount its products. If we fear intellectual self-assertiveness, we may mute our intelligence and suppress the best within us.

How can we counter the passivity generated by self-doubt? The best way to grow is to study success, identify with what successful people do that is different from what unsuccessful people do, then work at practicing those distinctive behaviors. Here are some of the basic steps I taught Theodora.

Make notes on your ideas as soon after they occur to you as possible. One of the most valuable assets an ambitious person can have is a notebook, kept nearby at all times, including beside your bed at night. If an idea occurs to you that you feel is promising or interesting, write it down immediately, in as much detail as you can. This is important because many people have been struck by an exciting idea that they did not record and soon forgot. I suspect everyone has known this experience. Successful people *take their ideas seriously.* People who are not yet successful can emulate this practice. Do not trust your memory, no matter how enthusiastic you feel in the moment.

Of course many ideas occur to us that, on reflection, we choose not to pursue, perhaps because at a later date they seem less impressive, or because they require more effort than we care to expend, or because they lie outside the sphere of our most important interest. But some ideas will be right for us, and those are the ones we need to cultivate.

When we have an idea we believe can be useful for the organization where we work, we need first of all to think it through in some detail. And then:

Identify possible objections and have answers for them.

Enroll associates in your vision—to gain allies for it. (To protect against ideas being stolen, it's often wise to write a memo to the boss at this point, outlining what one is doing.)

Identify what your boss would have to know in order to have a considered reaction to your proposal.

Learn how to prepare a proposal clearly, succinctly, and convincingly—how to "sell" your idea.

In addition to the steps outlined, we need one practice above all: perseverance. We may have to fight the same battle many times, with different people in the organization, before we see our vision executed.

Even if we do everything right, we will not necessarily win with our first idea. We may have to submit many ideas before our first victory. The ability to persevere is a hallmark of high achievers.

CHAPTER EIGHTEEN

Experimenting in Intimacy

Ellen and Paul had reached an impasse in their relationship. They loved each other yet seemed incapable of communicating without friction. They had been married six years. Ellen was afraid of confessing her fears when Paul seemed remote and withdrawn. Paul was afraid of confessing how much he loved and needed her, lest he feel too "weak." Unwilling to share their vulnerabilities, they shared their defensiveness instead. When Ellen spoke, her manner was often brittle and hurtful. When Paul answered, his manner was often aloof and detached. Sometimes they said cruel things to each other.

Now they had reached a point where they were hardly speaking at all.

I gave them a homework assignment that I call "an experiment in intimacy." I have used it many times in my practice when counseling couples. Here is what I asked them to do: They were to spend twelve hours together in the same room, entirely alone. No books, no television, no phone calls; not even any walks outside. No distractions of any kind. And no naps during this twelve-hour session, either. They were to arrange for someone to take care of their children for the day.

Ideally, I said, the experiment should be conducted in a hotel or motel room where they could get room service, so no time would be spent on preparing meals. Except for going to the bathroom, they were to remain together at all times.

They must agree that no matter what either of them says, neither will leave the room—and there will be no physical violence. They could sit for several hours in absolute silence if they chose to, but they must remain together.

They would be free, during these twelve hours, to talk about anything they wished, provided it was personal. It could be about themselves or about their relationship. But no talk of work, the children's schoolwork, redecorating the living room, or any other such subject. The focus must remain on themselves.

The premise behind this assignment is that, when all avenues of escape are closed off, people will often experience real breakthroughs in communication. As the hours pass, they find themselves talking from a deeper and deeper place within themselves.

Ellen was excited by the assignment, while Paul was somewhat anxious at the prospect.

"Twelve hours?" he asked, gulping.

"You mean," I laughed, "you married her for life, but twelve hours is too long to be alone with her?"

What happened with Ellen and Paul was fairly typical. They checked into a hotel in the morning and committed to staying with the experiment from 10 A.M. to 10 P.M. "no matter what." For the first hour or so, they felt a bit shy and awkward, made jokes, questioned the mental stability of their therapist—and avoided real personal contact. Then Ellen said something that annoyed Paul, and then he said something that annoyed her, and then they quarreled for a while, and then they made up. Over lunch they felt warmer with each other—and after lunch proceeded to make love. Because there was no time pressure, their love-making session lasted a good deal longer than usual and was exceptionally enjoyable for them both. They felt much closer and agreed that the experiment seemed to be a good idea—so much so, Paul suggested, that perhaps they could cut the day short and go to a movie. But they remembered their commitment to remain in the room for twelve hours. It was now 2:30 in the afternoon. Seven-and-a-half hours to go. And now the real experiment began. They had quarreled, they had eaten, they had made love. Now only one option seemed left: to talk about their feelings. And talk they did, as they forgot the "artificiality" of the situation and kept moving to deeper levels of honesty and intimacy—because there was no place else to go.

Ellen talked about the fear that was masked by her anger, and Paul talked about the fear that was masked by his remoteness. They talked about how scared they were of losing the other's love. They talked about things that had happened in the relationship that had hurt them. They talked about the ways they retaliated. They talked about what they wanted from the relationship and rarely got. They wept, and held each other, and reconnected with what had drawn them together in the first place. Then they fell into an argument and pulled apart again. They looked at the clock. Two more hours to go. "Are we going to sit and glower at each other, or are we going to solve this?" asked Paul. Again they reconnected, this time on still a deeper level. They began to talk about feelings they had never shared before, some happy, some unhappy, as they gained courage to take risks with self-disclosure.

The following week in therapy, Paul announced exuberantly, "We're committed to doing this exercise once every six weeks until our marriage is fully back on track again. Man, when you close all the exits, and there's just the two of you, and twelve hours staring you in the face—it's incredible what can happen!"

Very rarely, when I propose this experiment, do both people greet the idea enthusiastically. There is always some anxiety. But I have seen couples with almost every kind of communication problem imaginable achieve some kind of significant breakthrough during the course of this marathon. Sometimes, not often, the first attempt ends in a debacle: there is more chaos and confusion than clarity and contact. I cannot think of a single instance, however, in which the second marathon did not break this impasse.

Only three times in the past twenty years can I recall couples who decided at the end of the twelve hours that their relationship was better ended. And if the session produced that kind of clarity, that too was a success.

One woman was so impressed by the results she obtained with her husband that she proposed to her mother, with whom she was having difficulties, that they spend twelve hours alone together, following the same rules. The result was a breakthrough in their understanding of each other.

Hearing of this in one of my therapy groups, another woman client decided that the experiment need not be confined to relationships in trouble—and proposed to her closest friend that they do the experiment together. In the course of it, they shared their appreciation of one another as they never had before. "We probably have spent hundreds of hours talking in restaurants, but we never talked about the things we said during those twelve hours," she reported. "Cut off from the world, cut off from everything, so much more becomes possible. Wouldn't it be fantastic to do this with every person in your life who's important to you?"

What I like about this experiment is that it is so simple. One does not have to give a lot of instructions. One only has to create a context in which intimacy can happen.

Is the idea frightening to some people? Of course. It is an invitation to step into the unknown. One cannot predict what will happen. The mistake would be to imagine otherwise. But it is hard to think of any value or importance that does not require some measure of risk.

I can imagine some readers saying, "The project sounds intriguing, but—twelve hours? Couldn't we do it for six?" Twelve hours it is, friends, if you really want to find out what this experiment can offer you. Your relationship deserves it.

CHAPTER NINETEEN

Choosing Happiness

Some years ago, I found myself thinking a good deal about the subject of happiness, and about the idea of not merely desiring happiness but making its attainment my conscious purpose. This was an idea that first hit me as I approached my sixty-first birthday, and I would like to share some things I've learned.

My most important teacher in this area has been my wife, Devers, who is the most consistently happy human being I have ever known. How she achieves this is part of the story I wish to tell.

There is a tendency for most people to explain feelings of happiness or unhappiness in terms of the external events of their lives. They explain happiness by pointing to the positives; they explain unhappiness by pointing to the negatives. The implication is that events *determine* whether they are happy. I have always suspected that our own attitudes have far more to do with how happy we are than any external circumstances. Today, research supports this view.

Take a woman who is basically inclined to be happy, meaning that she feels happiness is her natural state and is happy a significantly greater amount of the time than she is unhappy. Let some misfortune befall her—the loss of a job, or a marriage, or being hit by some physical disability—and for some time she will suffer. But check with her in a few weeks or months, or a year later (depending on the severity of the problem), and she will be happy again.

In contrast, take a woman who is basically inclined to be unhappy, who feels unhappiness is more natural than joy, and who is unhappy a significantly greater amount of the time than she is happy. Let something wonderful happen to her—getting a promotion, inheriting a lot of money, falling in love with a wonderful man—and for a while she will be happy. But check with her a little later down the line, and very likely she will be unhappy again.

Research also tells us that the best predictors of a person's disposition to be happy are (1) self-esteem and (2) the belief that we ourselves, rather than external forces, are the most significant shapers of our destiny.

I have always thought of myself as an essentially happy person and have managed to be happy under some fairly difficult circumstances. However, I have known periods of struggle and suffering, as we all have, and at times I felt there was some error I was making and that not all of the pain was necessary.

I began to think more about Devers's psychology. When I met her I thought that I had never met anyone for whom joy was more her "nature." Yet her life had not been easy. Widowed at twenty-four, she was left to raise two small children with very little money and no one to help her. When we met, she had been single for almost sixteen years, had achieved success in a number of jobs, and had never spoken of past struggles with any hint of self-pity. I saw her hit by disappointing experiences from time to time, saw her sad or muted for a few hours (rarely longer than a day), then saw her bounce back to her natural state of joy without any evidence of denial or repression. Her happiness was *real*—and larger than any adversity.

When I would ask her about her resilience, she would say, "I'm *committed* to being happy." And she added, "That takes self-discipline." She almost never went to sleep at night without taking time to review everything good in her life; those were typically her last thoughts of the day. I thought that this was important.

Then I thought of something I had noticed about myself. And that was, as I sometimes joked, that with every decade my childhood kept getting happier. If you had asked me at twenty or at sixty to describe my early years, the report would not have been different about the key facts, but the *emphasis* would have been different. At twenty, the negatives in my childhood were in the front of my mind, so to speak, and the positives were at the back; at sixty, the reverse was true. As I grew older, my perspective and sense of what was important about those early years *changed*.

The more I studied and thought about other happy people I encountered, the more clear it became that happy people process their experiences so that, as quickly as possible, positives are held brighter in the foreground of consciousness and negatives are held dimly in the background. This is essential to understanding those people.

But then I was stopped by this thought: none of these ideas are entirely new to me. At some level they are familiar. Why have I not implemented them better throughout my life? Once I had asked the question, I knew the answer. Somehow long ago I had decided that if I did not spend a significant amount of time focused on the negatives in my life, the disappointments and setbacks, I was being evasive, irresponsible toward reality, not serious enough about my life. Expressing this thought in words for the first time, I saw how absurd it was. It would be reasonable *only if there were corrective actions I could be taking that I was avoiding taking.* But if I was taking every action possible, then a further focus on negatives *had no merit at all.*

If something is wrong, the question to ask is: Is there an action I can take to improve or correct the situation? If there is, I take it. If there isn't, I do my best not to torment myself about what is beyond my control. Admittedly, this last is not always easy.

The past few years of my life have been the most consistently happy I have ever known, even though it has been a time of considerable external stress. I find that I deal with problems more quickly than in the past, and I recover more quickly from disappointments.

One of the best ways I know to implement these ideas is to begin each day with two questions: *What's good in my life?* and *What needs to be done?* The first question keeps us focused on the positives. The second reminds us that our life and well-being are our own responsibility.

The world has rarely treated happiness as a state worthy of serious respect. And yet, if we see someone who, in spite of life's adversities, is happy a good deal of the time, we should recognize that we are looking at a spiritual achievement—and one worth aspiring to.

APPENDIX

Was Ayn Rand a Feminist?

(*Author's note:* A word of explanation is needed concerning the inclusion of this essay in this book. In 1991 the *New York Times* published the results of a survey undertaken by the Library of Congress in collaboration with the Book-of-the-Month Club. The purpose was to learn which books had had the greatest impact on American readers, which books had, in effect, produced life-changing experiences. The Bible was number one. Ayn Rand's *Atlas Shrugged* was number two. More people reported being profoundly influenced by this novel than by any other book, with the one exception noted. Because the novel has sold in the millions worldwide, and its heroine has been a role model for countless women, I found Rand's perspective on women and feminism of particular interest in the context of this book. A second reason for including it is that doing so allowed me to relate issues of self-esteem to certain strains of contemporary feminism.)

When I am asked about Ayn Rand and feminism, I often find myself thinking of two incidents in *Atlas Shrugged* involving Dagny Taggart, the heroine of Rand's novel.

Here is the first. "She was twelve years old when she told Eddie Willers that she would run the railroad when they grew up. She was fifteen when it occurred to her for the first time that women did not run railroads and that people might object. To hell with that, she thought—and never worried about it again."[1]

In the second incident, Dagny is an adult. "Lillian moved forward to meet her, studying her with curiosity. . . . [S]he found it strange to see Dagny Taggart wearing an evening gown. It was a black dress with a bodice that fell as a cape over one arm and shoulder, leaving the other bare; the naked shoulder was the gown's only ornament. Seeing her in the suits she wore, one never thought of Dagny Taggart's body. The black dress seemed excessively revealing—because it was astonishing to discover that the lines of her shoulder were fragile and beautiful, and that the diamond band on the wrist of her naked arm gave her the most feminine of all aspects: the look of being chained."[2]

Taken together, these two passages illustrate the complexity, and perhaps the ambiguity, of Ayn Rand's view of women.

She was always pleased when someone told her she "thought like a man." And yet, when asked if she would have preferred to be born a man, she invariably answered, "God no! Because then I'd have to be in love with a woman!"

I never thought this was funny, and she always insisted it was not her intention to be funny. But if she was serious, what were the implications of what she was saying? If she was putting down women, she was putting down herself. This inference was unavoidable.

On more than one occasion I remarked to her that while there were several heroic male characters in *Atlas Shrugged*, there was only one truly outstanding woman. "Why were there not more variants of the heroic woman in the story?," I asked. I recall her once chuckling and answering, "That didn't interest me. And, after all, this is *my* fantasy!"

Ayn Rand was a ferociously intellectual, proudly self-assertive powerhouse of independence who described herself as a "man-worshipper." To anyone who might imagine that this entailed a contradiction, she would say, "Check your premises."

The heroines in her novels are indifferent to convention, deeply self-confident, guiltlessly sexual, and, in the case of Kira Argounova in *We the Living* and Dagny in *Atlas*, the equal of any man in energy and ambition. None of them are mothers, and there is nothing discernibly maternal in their characterizations. Motherhood (and fatherhood) hardly exist in the universe of the novels. Rand herself never considered having children. (She told me that when she was a very young girl she wrote a story about a woman who had to choose between saving the life of her husband or her child—and chose to save her husband, with Rand's clear approval.) In her novels, her heroines' intense femininity is grounded in their reverence for *man*. Their attitude is almost primordial, for all their intellectuality, and I say without criticism that this is one of the factors that make Rand's women so interesting.

Rand often spoke enthusiastically about the legend of Brunhilde, a warrior-woman able to defeat any man in combat, who swore she would give herself only to the man who could prevail against her—which Siegfried, overcoming every obstacle, alone was able to do. Kira, Dominique Francon (*The Fountainhead*), and Dagny are *spiritual* warriors, unimpressed by most of the men they meet, and lonely for their Siegfried—the one man strong enough to "conquer" them. He was strong enough, let it be emphasized, not in muscles or wealth but in intellect, self-esteem, and character. And by "conquer," Rand meant inspire them to sexual/romantic surrender.

Once, when asked why she used such a word as "surrender," Rand answered that one should look at human anatomy and the nature of sexual intercourse.

She no doubt would have agreed with Camille Paglia's observation that man is contoured for invasion, woman for receptivity. Happy, even aggressive, receptivity is still a different experience than male thrusting. In the context in which Rand used it, "surrender" was emphatically not a negative word but a positive one. It was associated with admiration and trust.

As far as her view of women and of human rights is concerned, Rand's work is entirely compatible with the dominant direction of nineteenth-century feminism. Historically, feminism was born, not as a demand for special entitlements provided by means of political coercion, but for equal treatment with men before the law. These feminists did not view *men* as the enemy, nor capitalism, but *government.* Their battle was with the state and with the traditional, religious idea of woman as man's subordinate. These women were individualists who fought to be treated as such, that is, treated as *persons.* Rand's philosophy, Objectivism, holds that sexism, like racism, is a form of biological collectivism, and therefore Objectivism would have entirely supported the demand of nineteenth-century feminists for equal rights before the law, such as the right to vote, or to own property in one's own name, or to have legally unimpeded access to the marketplace.[3] In addition, women historically have been taught that self-sacrifice is their noblest duty. Objectivism opposes the entire notion of human sacrifice, whether the sacrifice of self to others or others to self. It insists that human beings be treated as ends in themselves, not as means to the ends of others. In upholding an ethics of rational or enlightened self-interest, Objectivism champions a woman's right to live as a free, independent entity. Finally, Rand's novels offer powerful role models of autonomous, self-assured, and self-assertive females who have been sources of inspiration to countless numbers of women. Looked at from the perspective of nineteenth-century individualist feminism, there is much in Rand to embrace and be enthusiastic about.

Further, it is worth remembering that in almost every part of the world and throughout virtually all the centuries behind us, women have been regarded, and have been taught to regard themselves, as the inferior of men. Some version of woman-as-inferior is part of the "cultural unconscious" of just about every society we know of—and in the "cultural *consciousness*" as well. Women's second-class status is a pronounced aspect of every brand of religious fundamentalism—be it Jewish, Christian, Islamic, or Hindu. It is at its most virulent in societies dominated by religious fundamentalism, such as modern Iran. Rand's writings could not possibly be more antithetical to this perspective in every conceivable respect. It is no accident that the most frenzied attacks on her books have come from religionists. A rejection of the religious vision of life is present on every page, implicitly when not explicitly. Her books are a celebration of life on earth and of the glories possible to humans *in this world.* And her women are no less unconventional than her men, in outlook, personal authority, and self-esteem. Paraphrasing a line from *The Fountainhead,* her books are a defiant *No* flung in the face of many of our traditions. So here, too, we can see in what way her work would support the aspirations of individualist feminism.

However, when we consider some of the strains of "feminism" that have emerged in the last two decades, the story is entirely different. Rand was a champion of reason, individualism, self-responsibility, independence—and capitalism. The left wing or "radical" feminism of the nineties sees reason, logic, and science as a "male conspiracy" to oppress women. Indeed, its most extreme exponents have virtually declared war on Western civilization, which they characterize as a product of "dead white males." All the basic premises of "radical" feminism entail collectivism and statism. It sees man—and capitalism—as the enemy, and the government as its agent, ally, and protector (when officials support its social agendas; otherwise, they are just another group of blind or oppressive males). It seeks not freedom but, in many contexts, *escape from freedom*—evidenced by the fact that it often looks to political coercion as the means to advance its aims, whether through affirmative action or tax-supported day-care centers or every kind of regulation of business activity imaginable, including regulation of speech. Its basic portrait of woman is of woman-as-victim, not as strong and self-responsible. Its basic portrait of man is of man-as-oppressor. The act of sex, even between people who are married and in love, is sometimes described as rape (see, for example, Andrea Dworkin). These are ideas with which more and more young college women are being indoctrinated.[4]

Granted that this type of feminist has never represented more than a small minority. More moderate varieties of feminism do exist, which do not set themselves against man or Western civilization. Even among today's more mainstream feminists, however, there is a strong tendency to look to the state as women's rescuer, thereby implying that women cannot flourish in a condition of freedom but are children requiring special protection. And unfortunately, it is the more extreme anti-male, anti-capitalism, anti-Western civilization, anti-reason-logic-and-science version that has achieved dominance in our educational centers and in the media. This is made clear in appalling detail in Christina Hoff Sommers's superb study, *Who Stole Feminism?*[5] The new form of Marxist class warfare is sex warfare— this is the social contribution of "radical" feminism.

There is nothing in the philosophy of such feminism that Rand would not despise. It is the antithesis of nineteenth-century individualist feminism. As to the extreme wing of these modern feminists, it would be quite in character for them to declare that "Ayn Rand was not a woman" or, at any rate, "a traitor to her sex," to quote Susan Brownmiller's indictment in *Against Our Will: Men, Women and Rape*.[6]

I want to pick up two themes alluded to earlier and relate them to Rand's view of women: her description of herself as a "man-worshipper" and her line in *Atlas* about " . . . the most feminine of all aspects: the look of being chained."

To begin with, there were two different senses in which she used the expression "man-worshipper." The first is explained in her introduction to the twenty-fifth anniversary edition of *The Fountainhead*, where she writes of man-worship as reverence for man at his highest potential.[7] Here, she clearly means "man" in the generic sense that includes woman.

However, in other contexts it is clear that she identifies femininity with man-worship understood as hero-worship of the man, assuming the particular man is worthy of it. It is easy to misunderstand her on this point because she never fully articulated what she meant and because in her novels her heroes treat the woman they love with unreserved respect, admiration, adoration, and "worship." There is no hint of inequality in their view of one another, no suggestion of the man "looking down." Her concept of romantic love entails passionate *mutual* admiration at the center of the relationship. It is hard to think of another novelist in whose work this vision is dramatized so powerfully.

I recall a conversation I had with her in the early years of our relationship, when she was expounding on her idea of feminine hero-worship. I was in my twenties at the time. I asked her: "Don't men worship women? I mean, the women they love?"

"Oh, I suppose so, but that's not how I would think of it. By 'worship,' I mean our highest capacity for admiration, reverence, looking up. I see man as superior to woman, and . . . "

"Oh, Ayn," I protested. "You don't. You're joking!"

"I am not joking," she answered seriously.

"Superior in what? Intelligence? Creativity? Moral worth?"

"No, of course not. In spiritual or intellectual matters the sexes are equal. But man is bigger, stronger, faster—better able to cope with nature."

"You mean, at a purely physical level?"

"The physical is not unimportant." Later, I often heard her reiterate this point.

I would return to this issue more than once, because I did not feel fully comfortable with her point of view. I did not like the language of "inferior" and "superior" applied in any way to men and women as such. Yet I was intrigued to discover, and thought it important, that many of the most independent, strong-minded women I met shared Ayn's perspective.

Ayn would smile good-naturedly at my evident bafflement over this issue. I understood, of course, that she was not talking about men in general but man at his highest, man the abstraction—the masculine principle. Once she said to me, as if to make the issue clear once and for all, "Don't you understand that a truly strong woman *wants* to see man as stronger? Certainly *her* man." When I asked why, she answered, "For the pleasure of surrendering."

I persisted, even though I felt a light bulb going on, "So in a way the issue is sexual?"

"Of course." Then she added, "And beyond that, the pleasure of being helpless at times, of laying down the burden of strength. In a way, that also is sexual. A woman can't do this with a man she doesn't look up to. Be honest. You understand me perfectly. This is exactly how you expect a woman to feel about you."

"Maybe so," I conceded reluctantly, "but I wouldn't try to defend my position philosophically."

"I would," she said brightly.

What was abundantly clear was that, at least in romantic contexts, Ayn *liked* the idea of man—*her* man—as "superior," if only in a very abstract sense.

I once asked her if she imagined that Galt or Francisco or Rearden, the three men in love with Dagny, ever thought of her as "inferior." *"Of course not,"* Ayn answered instantly. "It would not be proper for a man to think in such terms." But this did not alter her basic position.

Both as a lecturer and as a writer Ayn Rand loved to shock, and I do not doubt that some element of that motivation was operating when she wrote the line about "the most feminine of all aspects." As a metaphor, as poetry, she enjoyed the idea of woman being "ravished"—not by *any* man, to be sure, but by a hero. We know from Nancy Friday's *My Secret Garden* that millions of women are turned on by fantasies of being "ravished" or "overcome" by a dominant male figure. We know it also from the best-selling "romance" novels, the most commercially successful genre in publishing history. It is psychologically naive to pathologize all such fantasies, as many modern feminists so stridently do. (I will add that such contemporary individualist feminists as Joan Kennedy Taylor and Wendy McElroy do *not* pathologize these daydreams.) The fantasy is transcultural. It would be absurd to insist that it tells us nothing about the female psyche. I am emphatically not speaking of rape, which is a despicable crime and has been so regarded by ethical men and women everywhere.[8] I am speaking of the desire to surrender to, or be overcome by, a strong male in what is experienced as a romantic context. All women may not share this feeling; but we know that many women do, Ayn Rand among them. Neither Ayn Rand nor Brunhilde was weak, dependent, or a clinging-vine—and what would a Siegfried want with a weak, dependent, clinging-vine, anyway? Strength longs for the challenge of strength.

Describing the first sexual encounter between Dagny and Hank Rearden in *Atlas*, Rand writes: " . . . she knew . . . that her defiance was submission, that the purpose of all of her violent strength was only to make his victory the greater . . . "[9] No strong woman can experience herself fully—in the romantic sense—with a man she perceives as weaker than herself. No strong man can experience himself fully—in the romantic sense—with a woman he perceives as low in independence, personal authority, and self-assertiveness. If Aristotle was right in declaring that a friend is another self, how much more applicable is that idea to romantic love, to the relationship between a man and a woman. This is why you will not see a passionate love affair between a person of high self-esteem and one of low self-esteem; a difference of that kind has no erotic charge. The image of a woman "chained," in the passage quoted, is a metaphor intended to isolate woman in her sexual aspect only—and her desire to be "owned" by the man she loves. To take this image literally is to confess an extraordinary ignorance of man-woman relationships and the psychology of their intimate interactions.

Where did Ayn Rand stand with respect to feminism (a term she never liked)? A feminism that sees woman at her best as a heroic figure will find support and validation in Rand's writings. A feminism that defines woman as victim and man as her evil oppressor will see Rand as the enemy—because Rand sees woman not as weak but as strong, and because Rand sees romantic love between woman and man as an expression and celebration of their esteem for each other as well as their esteem for themselves.

Notes

1. New York: Random House, 1957, p. 51.
2. Ibid. p. 136.
3. Rand did not discuss "sexism" explicitly, but her position is logically implied by her discussion of racism in *The Virtue of Selfishness*, New York: New American Library, 1964, pp. 172–185. "Racism" was originally published in the September 1963 issue of "The Objectivist Newsletter," which she and I co-edited and co-published.
4. See, for example, Christina Hoff Sommers's *Who Stole Feminism?* (New York: Simon & Schuster, 1994) and Richard Bernstein's *Dictatorship of Virtue* (New York: Alfred A. Knopf, 1994).
5. Ibid.
6. New York: Simon & Schuster, 1976, p. 315.
7. Indianapolis, New York: Bobbs-Merrill, 1968, p. xii.
8. I once heard Rand tell someone at a lecture, "If you think the 'rape scene' in *The Fountainhead* is an actual rape scene, I suggest you read the passage again. If it is rape, it is rape by engraved invitation. No hero of mine would ever permit himself an actual rape, which would be contemptible."
9. p. 251.

References

Branden, N. *The Psychology of Romantic Love.* (New York): Bantam Books, 1981.

Branden, N. *How to Raise Your Self-Esteem.* (New York): Bantam Books, 1988.

Branden, N. *The Six Pillars of Self-Esteem.* (New York): Bantam Books, 1994.

Branden, N. *The Art of Living Consciously: The Power of Awareness to Transform Everyday Life.* (New York): Simon & Schuster, 1997.

Branden, N. *Taking Responsibility: Self-Reliance and the Accountable Life.* (New York): Fireside, 1997.

Branden, N. *Self-Esteem at Work: How Confident People Make Powerful Companies.* (San Francisco): Jossey-Bass, 1998.

Author's Note

For readers who wish to work on their self-esteem and pursue their study of the subject further, I recommend three books of mine:

The Six Pillars of Self-Esteem
Taking Responsibility: Self-Reliance and the Accountable Life
The Art of Living Consciously

All three books contain many exercises aimed at nurturing and strengthening self-esteem.

About the Author

With a Ph.D. in psychology and a background in philosophy, Nathaniel Branden is a practicing psychotherapist in Los Angeles, and, in addition, does corporate consulting all over the world, conducting seminars, worships, and conferences on the application of self-esteem principles and technology to the challenges of modern business. He is the author of many books, including *The Six Pillars of Self-Esteem, Taking Responsibility, The Art of Living Consciously,* and *Self-Esteem at Work: How Confident People Make Powerful Companies.* His work has been translated into fourteen languages and there are more than 3,000,000 copies of his books in print.

In addition to his in-person practice, he consults via the telephone worldwide. He can be reached through his Los Angeles office at:

P.O. Box 2609
Beverly Hills, CA 90213
Telephone: (310) 274-6361
Fax: (310) 271-6808
E-Mail: NathanielBranden@Compuserve.com
Website: http://www.nathanielbranden.net

Index

A

Abandonment: anxiety about, 65–66; jealousy and, 76; and success anxiety, 99

Acceptance. *See* Self-acceptance

Acclaim of others, self-esteem versus, 8–9

Action(s): fantasy versus, 47, 119; and happiness, 133; self-acceptance of, 21–22; translating ideas into, 117–121; trying different, 105–109

Affirmative action, 141

Against Our Will: Men, Women and Rape (Brownmiller), 143

Aloneness and alienation, owning strengths and, 27

Anger: destructive expression of, 81–82, 83; expressing, 81–85; fear of others', 89–90; as response to jealousy, 77; silent expression of, 83–85; steps for appropriate expression of, 82–83

Anxiety: about abandonment, 65–66; about success, 97–102; and defensiveness, 95–96

Aristotle, 147

Aspiration, 6

Assertiveness, 10, 39–44

Atlas Shrugged (Rand): heroic characters in, 137;

influence of, 135; view of women in, 136–137, 138, 143, 145–146, 147

Awareness. *See* Conscious living

B

Belonging, desire for, and disowning of strengths, 27

Boundaries, 111–115

Branden, N., 9, 19, 27, 64

Breathing: into anxiety, 65–66, 96, 101; into unwanted feelings, 20

Brownmiller, S., 143

Brunhilde, 138, 146–147

C

Career and workplace: building a, 117–121; conscious living and, 15–17; defensive behavior and, 88–90; integrity in, 57–58; purposeful living and, 46–48; self-esteem in, 117–121; success anxiety and, 97–98, 99

Caretaker role, 47–48, 70, 111–112

Challenge, 5

Changing of behavior, 105–110

Character assassination, 81–82

Childhood experiences, and defensiveness, 91, 92–93, 94

Comfort, self-esteem versus, 9

Commitment: to happiness, 131; to ideas, 117–121

Communication: about jealousy, 77–80; of anger, 81–85; defensiveness and, 87–96, 123; experiment in intimacy exercise for, 123–128; high versus low self-esteem and, 6–7

Conscious living, 9, 13–18; career and, 15–17; defensiveness and, 87–96; romance and, 14–15; self-assertion and, 40–41; sentence-completion exercise for, 17–18

Control, inner versus external sense of, 45

Courage, 48, 67, 101, 102

Criticism: defensiveness about, 87–96; sarcastic, getting husband to stop, 107–109

D

Dagny Taggart, 136, 137, 138

Day-care centers, 141

Defensiveness: as self-protective strategy, 87–95; steps to overcome, 95–96

Defiance, 42–43

Depression, as response to jealousy, 77

Different, trying something, 105–109

Disapproval, fear of, 55–56

Dominique Francon, 138

Dworkin, A., 142

E

Einstein, A., 109

Enlightened self-interest, 70, 140

Escape, closing off, for communication, 124, 126, 128

Ethical violations, integrity and, 57–58

Experiment in intimacy, 123–128; for communication with friend, 127–128; for communication with mother, 127; for couple communication, 123–126

F

Failure, fear of, 99

Fantasy: versus action on ideas, 119; versus action toward goals, 47; women's sexual, 146

Feelings: acceptance of unwanted, 19–20; respecting one's, 84–85

Feminism: Ayn Rand and, 135–148; individualistic, 139–141, 142, 146; radical, 141–143, 146

Flirting: jealousy and, 77–80; truthfulness about, 79–80

Fountainhead, The (Rand), 138, 141, 143, 148*n*.7

Friday, N., 146

G

Ginott, H., 85

Goals, taking responsibility for, 46–50

Government regulation, 141–142

Guilt feelings: and acceptance of unwanted thoughts, 20–21; and boundaries, 111–112; and fear of being selfish, 73

H

Happiness: choosing, 129–133; disposition for, 129–132; feeling worthy of, 100; versus focus on negatives, 132–133; relying on external circumstances for, 129–130

Homework assignments. *See* Experiment in intimacy; Sentence-completion exercises

Household chores, getting husband and children to perform, 105–107

How to Raise Your Self-Esteem (Branden), 19, 27

I

Ideas: acting on, 117–121; steps for taking seriously, 120–121

Infidelity: appropriate responses to, 77–80; and jealousy, 75–80; low versus high self-esteem responses to, 75–76

Integrity: consequences of failures of, 53; living with, 10, 53–59; and overcoming defensiveness, 96; relationship of, to mental health, 58; relationship of, to self-esteem, 53–55; sentence-completion exercise for, 58–59

Intimacy, experiment in, 123–128

J

Jealousy, 75–80; appropriate responses to, 77–80; causes of, 75–77; low versus high self-esteem responses to, 75–76; and self-esteem, 75

K

Kira Argounova, 137, 138

L

Living consciously. *See* Conscious living

Love: fear of loss of, 39–40, 99; feeling deserving of, 63–65; making unrealistic promises for, 55–56; self-esteem and, 63–70. *See also* Relationships; Romance

M

Male conspiracy, 141–143

"Man-worshipper," 143–144

Marx, G., 119
Masculine principle, 145
Masters and Johnson, 66
McElroy, W., 146
Men: attitudes of, towards
    self-esteem in women, 8;
    as oppressors, 141–143;
    socialization of, to per-
    form, 70; as superior to
    women, 138–139, 144–147
My Secret Garden (Friday), 146

N

New York Times, 135
No, inability to say, 55–56,
    113–114
Notebook, for writing down
    ideas, 120

O

Objectivism, 139–141
"Objectivist Newsletter,
    The," 148*n*.3
Ownership: of strengths,
    25–31, 40–41; of un-
    wanted parts of self, 19–24

P

Paglia, C., 139
Parents, inappropriate re-
    sponsibility-taking of, 114
Passivity, 33–34, 45, 120

Perseverance, 102, 121
Proactivity, 45–51
Promises and commitments:
    integrity in, 54–56; mak-
    ing unrealistic, in order to
    be liked, 55–56
Psychology of Romantic Love
    (Branden), 64
Purposeful living, 10, 45–51;
    examples of, 46–50;
    sentence-completion
    exercise for, 50–51; steps
    toward, 50
Purposes, 45–46; converting
    desires into, 50

R

"Racism" (Rand), 148*n*.3
Rand, Ayn, 135–148; femi-
    nism of, 136–148; hero-
    ines in novels of, 137–138,
    140; views of, on mother-
    hood, 137–138; views of,
    on women, 136–137,
    138, 143–147
Rape, 146, 148*n*.7
Reality, respect for, 87–88
Regeneration, 4–5, 6
Relationships: assertiveness
    and, 40–41; boundaries in,
    111–115; defensiveness

in, 90–92; experiment in intimacy exercise for, 123–128; fear of selfishness in, 71–73; integrity and, 56; jealousy and, 75–80; personal growth and, 29–30, 68, 72; purposeful living and, 48–50; sabotage of, 64, 65–68, 78; self-esteem and, 7–8, 63–70; self-responsibility and, 35; success anxiety and, 98; vulnerability and, 66–68. *See also* Love; Romance

Religious fundamentalism, 140–141

Resilience, 4–5, 6

Responsibility: boundaries and, 111–115; disowning strengths to avoid, 27; for formulating goals, 46; inappropriate, for others, 35–37, 111–115; for ownership of strengths, 28–29. *See also* Self-responsibility

Romance: Ayn Rand's view of, 138–139, 143–147; consciousness and, 14–15; jealousy and, 75–80; self-esteem and, 63–70. *See also* Love; Relationships

Romance novels, 146

S

Sabotage. *See* Self-sabotage

Self-acceptance, 9, 19–24; of positive strengths, 25–31; sentence-completion exercise for, 24; of unwanted feelings, 19–20; of unwanted past selves, 21–22; of unwanted thoughts, 20–21

Self-assertiveness, 10, 39–44; forms of, 41; versus hostile behavior, 39–40, 41–43; judgment in, 41–42; sentence-completion exercise for, 43–44

Self-concept, as destiny, 64–65

Self-efficacy, defined, 4

Self-esteem: anger and, 81–85; boundaries and, 111–112; career building and, 117–121; components of, 4; conscious living for, 9, 13–18; defensiveness and, 87–96; defined, 4; embracing strengths for, 25–31; empowering strategies for, 105–133; fallacious notions about, 53–54; fear of selfishness and, 69–74; and happiness, 100, 129–133; high versus low, 4–8; importance of, 3–12; as inner experience, 8, 34, 76; integrity and, 10, 53–59; jealousy and, 75–80; key practices for, 9–10; purposeful living for, 10, 45–51; and romantic love, 63–70; self-acceptance for, 9, 19–24, 25–31; self-assertiveness for, 10, 39–44; self-responsibility for, 10, 33–38; success anxiety and, 97–102; survival value of, 4–5

Self-expression, 6

Selfishness: accusations of, as tool of manipulation and control, 73; versus enlightened self-interest, 70; fear of, 69–74, 113–114; versus justice and objectivity, 74

Self-protection, defensiveness as, 87–96

Self-rejection: consequences of, 23, 28; socialization for, 23

Self-reliance, 33

Self-respect, defined, 4

Self-responsibility, 10, 33–38; avoiding, 114; sentence-completion exercise for, 37–38; versus taking responsibility for others, 35–37, 111–115. *See also* Responsibility

Self-sabotage: identifying, 101–102; of relationships, 64, 65–68, 78; success anxiety and, 97–102

Self-sacrifice, and fear of selfishness, 69–74

Sentence-completion exercises, 17; for conscious living, 17–18; for embracing strengths, 30–31; for integrity, 55, 58–59; for overcoming success anxiety, 101–102; for purposeful living, 50–51; for saying no versus saying yes, 113–114; for self-acceptance, 24; for self-assertiveness, 42–44; for self-responsibility, 36, 37–38

Setbacks, 4–5

Sex, Ayn Rand's views on, 138–139, 142, 145–147. *See also* Relationships; Romance

Sexism, Objectivist view of, 139–140, 148*n*.3

Sexual exclusivity, and jealousy, 75–76

Siegfried, 138, 146–147

Six Pillars of Self-Esteem, The (Branden), 9

Socialization: into caretaker role, 70, 113; for passivity, 33–34; against self-esteem of women, 10–11; for self-rejection, 23

Sommers, C. H., 142

Strengths: disowning of, reasons for, 27–28, 40–41; ownership of, 25–31; sentence-completion exercise for embracing, 30–31

Success, and acting on ideas, 117–121

Success anxiety, 97–102; recognizing, 100–102; self-sabotage and, 97–102; sentence-completion exercise for, 101–102; unconscious, 99–100

Surrender, of women to men, 138–139, 145, 146–147

T

Taylor, J. K., 146

V

Virtue of Selfishness, The (Rand), 148*n*.3

Vulnerability, 66–68

W

We the Living (Rand), 137

Who Stole Feminism? (Sommers), 142

Winners, 118

Withdrawing: as expression of anger, 83–85; as response to jealousy, 77, 78

Women: Ayn Rand's view of, 136–148; fear of selfishness in, 69–74; indispensability of self-esteem to, 5; socialization of, anti-self-esteem, 10–11; socialization of, for disowning power, 28, 33–34; socialization of, to be caretakers, 70, 113; view of, as inferior to men, 138–139, 144–147